T0273566

PRAISE FOR HOCKEY CONFIDE...

"I believe the mental part of hockey and positive thinking are very important. Isabelle has provided interesting and helpful insights."

JAROME IGINLA, *NHL, Colorado Avalanche, all-star, Canadian World Junior, World Cup, and World Championship team*

"I feel confident that this book can be beneficial to various hockey players, coaches, and families of players who deal with adversity at all levels."

GUY CHARRON, *NHL, formerly Detroit Red Wings, former head coach of the Kamloops Blazers*

"Isabelle's book will be so helpful to players struggling with all the emotions of being on a team."

MARK KACHOWSKI, *NHL, formerly Pittsburgh Penguins*

"The tools found in this book will help grow your confidence and equip you to be mentally tough in big-game situations."

RILEY NASH, *NHL, Boston Bruins*

"When you can link the mind to the ability to perform, you create a winner. Izzy creates winners!"

DR. MATT JAMES, *international speaker and educator*

"Isabelle delivers rapid results with integrity and passion."

DR. JOHN RYAN, *communication and transformation trainer*

"Isabelle Hamptonstone combines a sound foundation in human behavior with a keen awareness of the human condition ... Her passion is contagious!"

DR. PATRICK ROSS SCOTT, *trauma recovery specialist*

HOCKEY
CONFIDENCE

HOCKEY
CONFIDENCE

TRAIN YOUR BRAIN TO **WIN** IN HOCKEY AND IN LIFE

ISABELLE HAMPTONSTONE, MSc

GREYSTONE BOOKS

Vancouver/Berkeley/London

Greystone Books Ltd.
greystonebooks.com

Cataloguing data available from Library and Archives Canada
ISBN 978-1-77164-201-9 (pbk.)
ISBN 978-1-77164-202-6 (epub)

Editing by Shirarose Wilensky
Proofreading by Lana Okerlund
Cover and text design by Jennifer Griffiths
Cover photograph by iStockphoto
Printed and bound in Canada on FSC® certified paper by Friesens.
The FSC® label means that materials used for the product
have been responsibly sourced.

Greystone Books thanks the Canada Council for the Arts, the British Columbia
Arts Council, the Province of British Columbia through the Book Publishing Tax
Credit, and the Government of Canada for supporting our publishing activities.

The information contained in this book is not intended to serve as a replacement
for professional medical or legal advice. Any use of the information in this book is
at the reader's discretion. The author and publisher specifically disclaim any and
all liability from the use or application of any information contained in this book.

Canada

Greystone Books gratefully acknowledges the xʷməθkʷəy̓əm (Musqueam),
Sḵwx̱wú7mesh (Squamish), and səlilwətaɬ (Tsleil-Waututh) peoples on
whose land our Vancouver head office is located.

For Jean-Pierre
Thank you for teaching me two
powerful lessons:

Those who appear to have the most
confidence are sometimes

those in most need of help to develop
their confidence.

We never really know what another
person is dealing with,

so always, whenever possible,

be kind.

It is always possible.

CONTENTS

FOREWORD

IN 2005, after coaching athletes of both genders, young and old, I became a coaching mentor. I'd played for Team Canada and won a Stanley Cup with the New York Rangers, and then another with the Dallas Stars. I'd had experience winning as a coach as well, and I was looking for another way to give back to the sport that had brought me so much joy, learning, and opportunity.

When my generation was young, a large part of parenting centered around the kitchen table. Typically, dads went to work and moms would be at home. A lot of positive conversations happened during the times when Mom would meet with her friends at home for coffee around the kitchen table. The moms shared ideas and mentored each other. When Dad got home, he and Mom discussed those ideas and supported each other to become better parents. We don't have as many opportunities like that anymore.

Similar to parents, coaches require their own "kitchen table time." As a mentor, I discovered just how challenging it is to get hockey coaches together to exchange ideas and brainstorm solutions to help their athletes develop confidence. In my personal experience, developing my own confidence affected my ability to be successful. The best help we can give our players is to provide them with the opportunity to develop their hockey confidence so that they can become their own best friend and develop the personal skills that will last them a lifetime!

This book focuses on the needs of players who are looking for tools and solutions for the challenge of developing hockey confidence. It is a valuable resource for anyone interested in high-performance hockey, and it's also a valuable tool for self-development.

I am thrilled to support Izzy's work and help her build a legacy of providing exceptional resources to help hockey players, and their coaches and families.

Enjoy reading this book and building your own hockey confidence!

DOUG LIDSTER
Stanley Cup champion, Canadian Olympic hockey team,
NHL coach

INTRODUCTION

HOCKEY CONFIDENCE: YOUR KEY TO WINNING

Playing the Game of Your Life

PICTURE THIS...

Your heart is pounding.

The crowd is exploding, screaming your name.

Again and again, you hear your name—it becomes an anthem.

The anthem gets louder. The sound vibrates through your chest. It becomes a war cry.

The clock is running down. The team is watching you, trusting your every move.

You are in complete control. This is *your* time. The opposition is nothing more than a mere distraction.

You feel your heart banging against your rib cage. You are sucking in air. You are smiling.

You smell the sweat that's built up over the years seeping out of your hockey gear, its presence somehow reassuring.

You. Are. Beyond. Confident.

You inhale the frozen air coming off the ice. It reminds you of all the years you've spent flying from one end of the rink to the other. This is *your* ice.

You are solid, stable, balanced. Ready to take off.

You see the image of a panther in your mind's eye—dangerous, fully focused, and ready to explode at any second with controlled aggression.

This is your time.

This is your game.

You are playing the game of your life!

Then, in the time it takes to power a puck from one end of the ice to the other, you hear,

"What the hell did you do that for?! You are an *idiot!*"

What?!?

Within seconds, that hockey dream is now your worst nightmare.

The puck turns over. The other team is running away with your vision, your mission, your future.

The blow is painful. You snap right back down to earth—*bang!*

All too quickly, the game is over. Your dreams lie smashed on the ice. Your heart is aching. Your head is pounding.

You hear the crowd... complaining.

You smell the grease of the fast-food concession and it turns your stomach.

Your eyes glaze over and you can't even see your own stick clearly.

So near, and yet so far...

Just when you felt you were finally getting to the stage where you could be confident, trust your own instincts, and feel trusted, you lost it all. So near, and yet so far, the pain of defeat kicks in. You are right back at square one, lost and

This is your time. This is your game. You are playing the game of your life!

searching. Searching for the one thing that will transform your game, the one thing that will make you act out of faith in your own ability and not fear that you will mess up.

If only that fleeting feeling of confidence could last more than just a few seconds.

Searching for Solutions to Self-Doubt

HERE'S A QUESTION for you. Do you feel you would be a better hockey player if you had more faith in yourself when things went wrong? If you had more confidence? NHL all-star Jarome Iginla thinks so. He says: "Confidence is a big part of everybody's game."[1]

Do you agree? Is confidence a big part of your game? Perhaps you have said to yourself, *Today I will play a better game and have more fun*. You may even have promised that you won't question yourself so much, that today is going to be better, that *you* are going to be better. Then the heavy old mind games come right back. If only you had a solution to the self-questioning, the self-doubt, the anxiety, the exhaustion, the anger, the sadness, the fear, the hurt, and the guilt...

Perhaps you saw yourself being a much better player. You may have committed heart and soul to raising your stats and getting better results. Then you found that your nervousness or anxiety got in the way of playing the game of your life.

Doesn't it sometimes get exhausting to be inside your head so much?

Perhaps you doubt yourself, question yourself, so much that you make stupid mistakes. Perhaps you've gotten frustrated with your coach or angry at your teammates as your mood crashes down.

Do you ever feel guilty after a game, feeling as if you have let down yourself or your family or your team? Does the fear that you might never reach your full potential grate on you? Perhaps you have felt that your progress has been one step forward and one step back. You get a taste for the good feelings, the good results... and then, like water through your fingers, that progress slips away.

Sometimes you may even have lost hope of ever making powerful, permanent change happen for you. And now you may be beginning to think that it has something to do with you.

If you have felt like this in any way, at any time, you need to know that there are hundreds—if not thousands—of hockey players who feel this way too.

Changing Your Life for the Better

HOW DO I know that other players sometimes feel the way you do? I work with them, day in and day out. I train them to find ways to help themselves get better results by strengthening their hockey confidence.

Know this now: You are not alone. If you have been experiencing these feelings, then I wrote this book so that you can help yourself.

DOESN'T IT SOMETIMES GET EXHAUSTING TO BE INSIDE YOUR HEAD SO MUCH?

I'm Isabelle Hamptonstone—call me Izzy. I am the confidence consultant for hockey players in the National Hockey League (NHL), Canadian Hockey League (CHL), and American Hockey League (AHL); Olympic competitors; hard-playing corporate presidents; and maverick CEOs. I've written this for you from my home in Sun Peaks, British Columbia, Canada, which is close to the home of Memorial Cup champions the Kamloops Blazers. I've experienced, time after time, how training the brain to develop and sustain hockey confidence can upgrade results and change lives for the better.

The lives of the hockey players I've worked with have changed, and so have the lives of the families that support them. Players tell me that having one thing they can do for themselves, every day, has given them a solid internal foundation of confidence. From that foundation have come their greatest scores in life.

Successful NHL players that I train have told me that they are inspired by their heroes and learn from the life lessons that their heroes' stories can teach them. This has helped them to raise their game and to perform better, both as players and as human beings. They have achieved happier and more successful lives, full of rich new realities.

Sadly, for every successful player I work with one-on-one, there are hundreds more who are struggling to become truly confident. Those struggling players are yearning and searching for a way to make permanent positive change happen. But somehow that change seems to slip right through their fingers. You bet they deserve success. And you can bet they want it badly. You know that they're trying, trying, trying—day after day after day—to do better. How do you know? You may have been there too.

That is why I wrote this book: to share knowledge so that you, too, can reap the rewards. It's also to provide tools and examples for the people who support you and to help turn you into a game changer. This book is designed to help you—to help you help yourself and get results. So here it is, a step-by-step page-turner of stories and solutions that addresses the fundamental key to your success in hockey: overcoming the mental block that is lack of confidence.

Learning from the Best

THIS BOOK CONTAINS a collection of powerful techniques that work consistently. Use the tools, learn from the stories, and develop your own powerful confidence to help you deal with stressful situations. As you'll see, some of the greatest hockey players in the world have used these very same action steps to change their game and their lives.

On our journey of profound personal development, we will be joined by some of the biggest names in hockey, and I'll share stories of some of the greats, including Wayne Gretzky, Doug Lidster, Scott Niedermayer, Shane Doan, Darryl Sydor, Jarome Iginla, and Mark Recchi. They were all determined to make powerful, positive change happen, and *they took action*. They stepped up. Their intention and the right actions produced results—and in some cases, Stanley Cup championships. The key to their success was finding the right tools to help them deal with tough situations, and then using them. You, too, can learn from the best, from players who really know what it is to be hockey confident.

> **Confidence is a big part of every-body's game.**
> JAROME IGINLA

Remember, great minds think alike. There is a phrase that many find inspirational: "Stand on the shoulders of giants," which suggests that we all would do well to learn from our heroes who have gone before us. This is especially true in hockey! They can show us how to deal with our challenges by telling us how they dealt with theirs.

This is your time, this is your game, and this is your life. Stand on the shoulders of the hockey giants and learn from the best. Reach higher, skate faster, get consistently confident, develop your focus and accuracy, and become the champion you were meant to be.

Here, in this book, is a wealth of ways to get better, together with stories of action to inspire and create hockey confidence. Nothing complicated—just a collection of powerful tools to catapult you forward and help you win from within.

Power up your performance by getting hockey confident.

Skate like the wind,
IZZY

ONE

TAKE RESPONSIBILITY FOR YOUR PROGRESS

Shift Happens

"Other famous men, those of much talk and few deeds, soon evaporate. Action is the dignity of greatness."

JOSÉ MARTÍ, Cuban revolutionary philosopher and author

WHEN YOU TAKE action, the right action, when you take one step a day in the right direction toward becoming more confident, strong, fit, fast, and accurate, you will get results. Those results may happen slowly at first, just as when you first stepped out onto the ice all those years ago. But you will quickly build momentum—first one foot, then the other; one thought, then another—and quickly you will see yourself making the shifts and changes you need to become a better person, a better player. A winner.

When you take the time to notice the positive changes you are making by taking these action steps, you supercharge the momentum of positive change—just as a fast-moving puck has more momentum when it's hit with twice the power. The shift in the right direction is happening.

Keep a journal, or a record on your smartphone, or write notes directly on the pages of this book so that you can look back and watch your success build. Doing this daily will sow the seeds of success in your mind. The more you do it, the more quickly you will become more powerful.

One NHL player, who started working with me back in his CHL days, has sent me one email a day, every day, for three solid years. With those emails, he is taking the time to acknowledge and share his successes, and to make the most of the good feelings that generates—every single day. Now that's what I call a player who is determined to be successful!

Do you know of anyone else who is prepared to take one action step a day to be more successful?

The Puck Stops Here

"Hockey's a funny game. You have to prove yourself every shift, every game. It's not up to anybody else."
PAUL COFFEY, second all-time NHL defenseman in career goals, assists, and points

THERE IS SOMETHING very special about the hockey players I work with who make it big. Yes, they are hardworking. Yes, they are determined. Yes, they take action. Yes, they love the game. And yes, they look forward to getting more powerful every day, both physically and mentally. But what's the biggest difference between the players who succeed and the ones who don't? In my experience, the players who succeed *take responsibility* for their results and their progress.

Listen carefully to the radio and TV interviews after an NHL game. Pay particular attention to players on the losing team and listen closely for the way they take responsibility for their actions. Good or bad, players who succeed hardly ever use the word *blame*. They do not blame their linemates, the quality of the ice, or the words of the coach. The greatest players know that ultimately the only people who can take full credit for their progress are the players themselves.

What's also important is that when we listen to those successful players talk about their upbringing, their home life, their family, their education—all their struggles and challenges—we learn something interesting from what they say and how they say it. Without fail, they never blame their life situation.

The most confident players—the ones who win consistently—hold themselves accountable. In spite of their problems and struggles, they take responsibility for what they have achieved, and *all* of them have had to deal with challenges along the way. Life challenges, like hockey pucks, will just keep coming right at you. It's how you deal with them that counts.

What does this mean to you? Is there something these players are doing that you can use, that will shift how you look at your progress? You bet.

Starting today, learn from the greats. Know that taking responsibility for your progress is the first step. It is the key to your success, in hockey and in life. Start *now* to develop the habit of being accountable and taking responsibility for what you do, how you do it, what you say, and how you say it. Yes, absolutely, there will be times when you'll kick your-self because what you said or did wasn't what you would do if you could start all over again. Here's the thing—we all mess up sometimes.

We All Mess Up

"Without mistakes, how would we know what we had to work on?"
PETER MCWILLIAMS, American self-help author

WE ALL WISH sometimes that we could take back our words or our actions—the ones that make us cringe when we think about them. It's how we act when we mess up that turns us into champions. We can make a conscious decision to take respon-sibility for our actions and our words. We can resolve right now to do better next time—and make sure that next time we do in fact do better.

The beauty of being human is that we are born to learn, develop, grow, and get better every single day. At every moment, our brains are developing more fully—we are learning more every second. It's a natural human state to be changing a little bit every day. By making the decision to change our actions and responses a little bit in the right way every day, we are guaranteed to become a better player and more confident playing the game of life, which means that we will inevitably taste success more regularly.

SUPERCHARGE THE MOMENTUM OF POSITIVE CHANGE—JUST AS A FAST-MOVING PUCK HAS MORE MOMENTUM WHEN IT'S HIT WITH TWICE THE POWER.

Here is an awesome piece of advice that has helped my players find the strength to stand up and be strong. A great guy in my village passed it on to me many years ago. Now I live my life by this advice, and it has helped my players develop their own sense of personal power.

Wilf Bennett is a hardworking man who has a great perspective on people. A former bull rider and author, he shared with me these words, based on an old proverb: "There are three kinds of people: those who make things happen, those who watch things happen, and those who ask, 'What happened?'" What a way to sort out those who step up when they mess up, those who talk about stepping up, and those who never step up!

You may already be the player who makes things happen, or you may want to be that player. The key here is to step up and take action. Be accountable for your actions, good or bad. Own them, and take responsibility for making progress.

You may be thinking, *Why is taking responsibility important for developing my hockey confidence?* Good question. Here's why:

Ask yourself, when you blame other people for your actions:

· Does it feel good inside? Does it really?
· Does it feel like a hit to your happiness?
· Do you feel like crap?
· Do you wish you could see yourself feeling better?
· Is your confidence sky-high afterwards?

It's okay—I know the answers, and now you do too. Putting the blame on other people prevents you from taking ownership of your part. When you take ownership of your actions, you take responsibility for upgrading your results. Start *now* to develop your confidence by taking responsibility for your actions and for your progress.

Let's take a look at the story of one NHL player who took personal responsibility for his decisions and actions and used it to develop his confidence before he even got to the NHL.

It's how we act when we mess up that turns us into champions.

First overall draft pick Nathan MacKinnon is an inspiring example of someone who makes things happen on the ice and takes responsibility for his actions. Nathan played hockey in his home province of Nova Scotia. He took responsibility to improve himself and his game and was a key factor in helping the Halifax Mooseheads come from behind in a crucial Memorial Cup game.

"He was the guy who competed all the time," says Halifax head coach Dominique Ducharme of his star forward's performance. "He made things happen, he was skating, he was hard on the puck, it was hard to get the puck from him, and obviously he was a big reason for our comeback."[1]

Nathan took responsibility for his progress and his success, and he helped his teammates by being fully committed to getting results. The Mooseheads went on to win the Memorial Cup, and Nathan was named most valuable player (MVP) of the tournament. Later, he became the youngest player ever to play a regular season game for the Colorado Avalanche.

Now let's see how taking personal responsibility for your decisions, actions, and progress develops into an action step that will set you on the path to building your inner strength and hockey confidence.

Setting Yourself on Fire

"You can't build a reputation on what you're going to do."
HENRY FORD, founder of the Ford Motor Company

THINK. WHICH PLAYERS do you admire the most? How did you hear about them? What happens when you watch them? How do you think it feels to be that successful? If they were unsuccessful, would you be admiring those players? Would you be watching them? Would you have even heard of them? Maybe not.

Do you think that their flame of success burned bright right from the very beginning... or is it possible that their success started small, just like a roaring fire always starts from a tiny spark? Do you suspect that over the years they chose to learn from the best, to grow and develop and find ways to get stronger—just like you? Absolutely! And you know what? They never stop learning.

It's important for all of us to remember this: *We all started somewhere.*

There may be times in our lives when we want to be further ahead than we are. Here's an action step that will help you move forward:

When are we at our strongest, our most confident, our most powerful? Is it when we are doing nothing to help ourselves? Probably not.

Yes, it's good to take a well-earned break and enjoy the rest and relaxation of time off. It's interesting, however, that after a huge amount of time out and relaxation, our brains get bored. We start to want to have things to do. It's simply human nature to want to take action, make progress, and get results.

Now we are developing the concept of fanning the flames of your success. You could fan the flames by taking action, such as getting to the rink more often or practicing against harder opponents to improve your shooting accuracy. You could set your determination on fire and plan your social life around hockey, to make the most of every minute on the ice. Action in the right direction creates results.

Is there more to success than this? Absolutely. Here is a very simple equation that I show my players. It illustrates the two key qualities that appear time and again in successful hockey players.

$$Intention + Action = Results$$

Fan the flames
of your own
success and take
responsibility for
your progress
by speaking to
yourself in a way
that encourages
you to do better.

Fuel yourself with the fire of great intentions. Focusing on a powerful outcome, and the actions you take, with this in mind will naturally get you there quicker.

One man who used his intentions to get results was Philadelphia Flyers player Bobby Clarke. Bobby had been diagnosed with type 1 diabetes at the age of 13. Some of the symptoms of diabetes can include feeling tired, thirsty, and very low energy. An NHL player with diabetes has a set of challenges to overcome that are as unique as they are potentially debilitating.

Bobby's intention was to be judged for his talent, not his condition. He didn't want to be known as "the diabetic athlete." Instead, he says, "I'm a hockey player that just happens to have diabetes... that's all! Judge me how I play hockey; don't judge me by my having diabetes."[2] He was clear about his intention, and he backed it up with his words and actions. He also became one of the best two-way forwards of all time.

Intention + Action = Results

So let's take a leaf from the book of Bobby's success and decide right here, right now, to take action. You get to decide your goals—your reasons for reading this book. Write down here the results you would like to see from using this book. What would you like to be, do, and have as a result of developing your own hockey confidence?

Here are some examples:

- I want to feel more confident.
- I want to be a stronger, more powerful hockey player.

- I want to hear good comments when people talk about my ability.
- I want to enjoy my sport more.
- I want to be more positive.
- I want to score more goals/make more saves.
- I want to have more fun when I play hockey.
- I want to be proud of my results.
- I want to be happy about how I conduct myself on and off the ice.

_____

_____

_____

_____

_____

Now set your intention for reading this book and improving yourself.

But wait—you just did! *Setting your intention* is simply deciding the outcome that you want ahead of time. So you've completed half of the success equation already!

Intention + Action = Results

Now, that you are clear on your goals and know what results you're looking for, the next step is—you guessed it—taking action. Hmmm...

Sometimes the thought of taking action can be overwhelming, so let's break it down into small steps. Today, and every day until you reach the end of this book, take one small action step—*every single day*—toward achieving your intentions. As Paralympic medalist Linda Mastandrea says, "What separates a winner from the rest of the pack is not raw talent or physical ability; it is the drive and dedication to work hard every single day and the heart to go after your dream, no matter how unattainable others think it is."[3] Start today. It's powerful to realize now that one small step a day in the right direction will take you directly along the path to your success.

It's important for all of us to remember this: *We all started somewhere.*

When you combine this practice with taking responsibility for setting those intentions and making those steps, the progress and results you achieve will be a credit to your determination and focus.

Intention + Action = Results

Reggie "the Riverton Rifle" Leach was a Stanley Cup champion with the Philadelphia Flyers and is the father of

Jamie Leach, another proud holder of a Stanley Cup honor. He knows a thing or two about what it takes to play hockey and what it took to help his son develop his hockey talents. Reggie, quoting humorist Arnold H. Glasow, says, "Success isn't the result of spontaneous combustion. You must set yourself on fire."[4] He takes responsibility for his own success and is prepared to take action and focus his intention to get the right results. He fans the flames of his own success.

Fanning the Flames of Success

"A mighty flame followeth a tiny spark."

DANTE ALIGHIERI, author of the *Divine Comedy*

DO YOU ALWAYS feel happy when you play hockey? Does it hurt sometimes? Is it possible that once you get off the ice you feel exhausted? Do you sometimes have to miss out on socializing with your friends or spending time with your family to go to hockey practice? In spite of all this, do you still find yourself wanting to enjoy playing hockey?

If your answer to the last question is yes, then you are already starting to fan the flames of your own success. How? You already know that no matter how hard the game, no matter how early the practice, no matter what you have to miss to get to training, somewhere deep inside there is always a part of you that wants to get back out on the ice. Sometimes you may feel tired and overwhelmed and worn out, but there is still something about the game that you enjoy and that will always draw you back for more.

You can fan the flames of your own success because *the initial spark of success is already there.* That is the spark of fun and love of the game. The following quotation from Gordie Howe inspires players who need to remember why they work so hard every day to become a better hockey player: "You've got to love what you're doing. If you love it, you can overcome any handicap or the soreness or all the aches and pains, and continue to play for a long, long time."[5]

Gordie Howe—"Mr. Hockey"—was the hockey phenom of his time. His long career, his scoring ability, his accuracy, and his physical strength set him apart from his peers. Born in 1928, Gordie still commands respect today, and hockey coaches often share his advice with their players.

To love your game is to find the fun in the game. That amplifies your level of confidence and helps you to be stronger. It's a good thing that you know now that you already have the spark in you. Now you get to fan the flames of your success.

If you want to fan the flames of your own success, choose today to take responsibility for being the driving force behind your own good mood. If you want more laughter and more spark in your life, decide to find ways to be fun to be around. Monique and Jocelyne Lamoureux, twin sisters and star players on the U.S. Olympic hockey team, often talk about the importance of keeping things fun while working out and playing hockey. "Show up and be fun,"[6] says Jocelyne. And when you do, you find the fun in your game. It's always there if you look hard enough. Use it to blaze bright and find ways to fan the flames of your success. Great players and great leaders blaze bright with powerful confidence.

Blazing Bright with Confidence

"A lot of people, when a guy scores a lot of goals, think, 'He's a great player,' because a goal is very important, but a great player is a player who can do everything on the field. He can do assists, encourage his colleagues, give them confidence to go forward. It is someone who, when a team does not do well, becomes one of the leaders."

PELÉ, the greatest footballer of all time

WHICH HOCKEY PLAYERS do you know who blaze bright and don't make a fuss? A number of players spring to mind. How is it that they don't have to say much, because the way they play does all the talking for them?

Of all the players out there who display calm and true leadership, one of the greats is Pittsburgh Penguins and Team Canada legend Sidney Crosby. When hockey fans watch Sidney and listen to him speak, they see and hear a hockey player who speaks with true *confidence*.

What do I mean by true confidence? People who are comfortable in what they do and how they do it, and in what they say and how they say it. A player who is comfortable playing his game and likes the results he gets when he plays. I'm describing a way of living and being successful that comes from acting with honor, dignity, and self-respect—and from taking responsibility for getting results that count.

There are people with true confidence all around us. It's the single-parent hockey mom who works hard every day to make sure the bills get paid and there's food on the table yet still finds time to drive her kid to the ice, day after day after day. It's the unassuming kid in the class who doesn't need to be the loudest person to feel that she deserves to be part of the group. It's the Sidney Crosbys of this world who play hockey with good intentions and determination, have respect for themselves and others, and take the right actions so that their play speaks for itself.

How can you develop your own true confidence? Good question. I'll share my personal inspiration with you. Over the years, I've heard or read words and seen pictures that inspire me and help me feel good. No matter where they come from, if they inspire me, I write them down. Then I read them, one a day, to provide a spark of inspiration and to fan the flames of success.

Perhaps you also enjoy it when someone shares a bit of advice that has worked for them and helps you feel strong. Here are a few words of inspiration that were spoken centuries ago by a wise man, the Buddha, and have been repeated often. He said, "If you cannot find the truth right where you are, where else do you think you will find it?" Buddha is explaining the importance of taking personal responsibility for our inner happiness, for our own results. This is an important and empowering philosophy. We can each learn to use it to help us get results. What's the truth that Buddha speaks of? Ultimately,

IF YOU CANNOT FIND THE TRUTH RIGHT WHERE YOU ARE, WHERE ELSE DO YOU THINK YOU WILL FIND IT?

BUDDHA

it's all down to each one of us, to take responsibility to learn, to grow, to develop, and to deal with challenges so that we can become more content and happy with ourselves.

It is true that we can try to find the answer to our challenges in our surroundings, in our families, in our hockey... and we may actually find solutions and happiness there for a short time. But unless we connect to that spark of joy that is always within us—no matter how small it is—we will not find the long-term happiness we truly desire. Helen Keller said it very well: "Happiness cannot come from without. It must come from within. It is not what we see and touch or that which others do for us which makes us happy; it is that which we think and feel and do."[7] One of the keys to being truly confident, content, and happy is to take personal responsibility for our own well-being.

Hockey Hall of Famer and four-time Stanley Cup champion "Terrible Ted" Lindsay played for the Detroit Red Wings and the Chicago Blackhawks. He says that one of the greatest lessons he ever learned about the power of taking personal responsibility came from his father. "When the Depression hit and he had to raise six boys and three girls, he took responsibility."[8] In the midst of a worldwide economic crisis, Ted's dad dug deep, making himself responsible for putting food on the table, clothes on his kids' backs, and shoes on their feet. He taught Ted how to be responsible for taking care of business and to value each and every opportunity.

Ted started his hockey career in skates borrowed from the husband of a family friend. They were way too big, but he loved them anyway. The happiness spark was always there, and Ted chose to blaze bright, even in borrowed hockey skates. He took responsibility for his inner happiness, and over time, the results came thick and fast. The guy who started playing in boots that were too big became the NHL's leading goal scorer, and that year, his team won the Stanley Cup. By then, the skates probably fit!

When we decide today that how we feel and how we act—and the results we get—are our own responsibility, we can begin to take ownership of every small step forward that brings us closer to our goals. This develops our ability to act from a feeling of true confidence. Ultimately, our sense of contentment and personal happiness will naturally blaze brighter.

Being Your Own Head Coach

"Ask yourself what makes you come alive. And then go and do that. Because what the world needs is people who have come alive."
HAROLD THURMAN, civil rights leader

SOMETIMES THAT GAME that used to bring us so much fun and personal reward doesn't feel so much like fun anymore. We feel fed up, and the outlook isn't good. Something in us says it's time to make a change. The good news is this is the perfect time to learn what's going on in our minds and become our own head coach.

Listen to the people around you when they talk about their goals. Take the time to notice if their words are about what they actually want. Perhaps they're really saying what they *don't* want. Here's the takeaway: the mind doesn't pay much attention to the *do* or *do not* part.

For example, if someone (that would be me) tells herself to stop thinking about chocolate, to forget about how it smells or how good it looks in the wrapper, her mind will focus on the word "chocolate." Now all she can think is, *Where is that bar of extra-dark I hid somewhere?* Hang on, I'll be right back. Mmm ... Okay, where was I?

Ah, yes, let's bring this back into the hockey arena. What if, just before a penalty shootout, the player keeps telling himself, *Don't miss this shot, don't miss this shot, don't miss this shot ...* What do you think his mind will be focusing on? His brain will be setting him up to *miss, miss, miss* the shot.

So what action do you need to take to be your own powerful head coach? Learn to monitor your self-talk.

Case Study: Powering Up the Play

"I think self-awareness is probably the most important thing toward being a champion."

BILLIE JEAN KING, tennis player and activist

OFTEN WE CAN reach a plateau and find ourselves unable to make a breakthrough, or we can even find that we no longer enjoy ourselves as much anymore—especially after many, many months of training and focus on a particular project. An incredibly talented golfer I worked with, Ryan Weatherall, learned that self-awareness could turn his game around. I trained Ryan to concentrate on how he spoke to himself, on his internal self-communication.

I had heard Ryan talk about what he *didn't* want when talking about his goals. He didn't want to *waste his time on the golf course*, he didn't want to *miss his shot*, he didn't want to *let his family down*, and he didn't want *all his hard work to go to waste*.

The trouble with Ryan was that his mind had to think about what he *didn't* want in order to focus on what he did want. Ryan's mind was overworked focusing on *wasting his time on the golf course, missing his shot, letting his family down,* and *all his hard work going to waste*.

Ryan had to discipline his mind to notice what he was doing when he spoke to himself. As psychologist Daniel Goldstein says, "I think self-discipline is something; it's like a muscle. The more you exercise it, the stronger it gets."[9]

When Ryan found the discipline to change his focus, when he became aware of the power of his own words, he enhanced his personal power. He says, "I struggled with mental focus throughout the round. I could often keep it together for sections of a round and score very well. When I would lose my focus, I often lost very good rounds or had a lot of making up to do. This season, after I have played 15 rounds or so, I must say I have been able to keep focused throughout. Through thick and thin if I hit a bad shot, I think back to our positive thinking and self-control. I get it back together quicker than ever. My mentality has never been stronger. It is amazing to feel at the top of my game all the time in all aspects of life.

"What is also quite impressive is that I am not the only one to notice the change. Upon my return home after my stay in B.C., I have had several long-term friends as well as my family notice a big change. For starters, I returned to my home course to play with my long-term coach, Bob, to kick off the season. I played very well but didn't realize that it was not only the score that was impressive that day! We went into Bob's office after the round to have a chat. The biggest thing on my mind was how my game was. All he could talk about was how well I managed the course and didn't let my typical frustrations come out in my game that day. He was amazed, and after thinking the round over, so was I!

"I have been able to have a very successful opening to my season, I have never scored this well, and I plan on keeping it up. Every day I go to the golf course, no matter what mood I am in, I know I can go low. I cannot wait for the future! There are big things coming this summer! I am ecstatic about finally reaching my full potential."

Words Have Wings, so Speak Good Things

"*I AM. Two of the most powerful words, for what you put after them shapes your reality.*"
ANONYMOUS

NOTICE WHAT YOU say to yourself.
Instead of saying:

- I will not miss this goal.
- I hope I don't mess up this shift.
- I must not embarrass myself in front of my team.
- I can't let my team/coach/family/self down.

Repeat in your mind, again and again:

- I'm going to score now.
- I will skate like the wind.
- I am going to make my team/coach/family/self proud.

You get the idea. Fan the flames of your own success and take responsibility for your progress by speaking to yourself in a way that encourages you to do better. Enjoy talking to yourself in a positive way. After all, when others say encouraging things to you, it feels good. Why not speak to yourself in the same way?

Let's take a look at another great way to upgrade how we can communicate with the mind and get better results.

Have you ever decided on a goal, and then tried and tried to achieve it, but it just never turned out the way you wanted? Many of my players have, too.

The solution to the challenge is to notice the words we are using. When we say we will try to do well in hockey, the word "try" has importance. It tells our mind to be prepared for two outcomes. When we use "try," we are telling our mind that we are just as likely to fail at the task as we are to succeed. It's a 50-50 mental energy split. In *Star Wars*, Yoda hit the nail on the head when he told Luke Skywalker, "Do or do not. There is no try."

Another way of putting this is an expression that I had when I grew up in Wales: "Pee or get off the pot" (that's the polite version!). It means do it or don't do it, but either way, get on with it! Decide to do something or decide not to do it. None of that in-between stuff is going to get you anywhere.

List your tries. Be aware of what you say to yourself and the impact of your self-talk. Over the next seven days, write down how often you use the word "try." For the next week, take a

---

Every time you find yourself using the word "try," find another way to declare positively what you want to achieve.

---

pen and a small piece of paper, and make a mark on the paper every time you say it, or keep a note of it on your smartphone.

Every time you find yourself using the word "try," find another way to *declare positively* what you want to achieve. This will shift your mental energy. For example, change: "I'll try to have a good game." to "I'm going to have the game of my life!" If you use this technique, day by day you will begin to communicate more effectively with and train the most powerful piece of equipment you will ever use—your own mind.

You will identify old self-defeating habits and replace them with new more powerful habits. With determination, practice, and repetition, and by taking responsibility for getting great results, come new and powerful habits. Rather than *trying* to have an amazing game, go ahead and *be determined* to have an amazing game.

Tips

1. Dedicate yourself daily to becoming more successful. Take one step a day toward your goals to build consistent results over time.

2. Take the time to notice the positive changes. When you take time to notice positive change, you supercharge its momentum.

3. Keep a written record so that you can look back and watch your progress build.

4. Take responsibility for your progress and results. The puck stops with you. Notice and model excellence in other players who hold themselves accountable and take responsibility in spite of challenges.

5. Decide today: Are you going to be the player who makes things happen, who watches things happen, or who asks, "What happened?"

6. Fuel yourself with the right intentions and *take action* to get results.

7. Find the fun in each day and be the driving force behind your own good mood. If you want more laughter in your life, decide to find ways to be fun to be around.

8. Focus on developing high-quality confidence by taking responsibility to deal with challenges, to learn, to grow, and to develop.

9. Be your own head coach by speaking to yourself in a way that encourages you to do better. Enjoy talking to yourself in a positive way.

10. Monitor your self-talk. Which words inspire you? Use them.

11. Be aware of the power of the word "try." Decide to do something or decide not to do something.

TWO

ANXIETY: ONE OF THE GREATEST TOOLS FOR YOUR SUCCESS

The Chattering Monkey of the Mind

"Practically everybody knows what it's like to feel anxious, worried, nervous, afraid, uptight, or panicky. Often, anxiety is just a nuisance, but sometimes it can cripple you and prevent you from doing what you really want with your life. But I have some great news for you: You can change the way you feel."

DAVID D. BURNS, Stanford University School of Medicine

WE ALL KNOW athletes who, with more confidence, could play so much better and enjoy their game so much more. Although they may have skill or natural talent, they question themselves, they doubt themselves. They make mistakes in games that they never would in practice, and they are harder on themselves than anyone else. It's as if they have a chattering monkey sitting on their shoulder, giving a running commentary on how well they are *not* doing. The monkey is constantly telling them that they are not good enough, and that monkey is causing mayhem in their mind, causing them to experience performance anxiety.

You know those players, the ones who find it hard to feel good about their game. No matter how their friends, families, and coaches do their best to help, somehow they still feel like they are a failure. Their game may have a strong physical and technical base, but that lack of confidence affects their playing, their happiness, and their state of mind.

And their greatest fears about failure come true. They don't get the results they expect of themselves. They feel frustrated and confused. They don't know how to get back to finding the fun in their game and getting the results they deserve. Their self-esteem becomes extremely low and affects the person they want to be. They don't look at themselves the way others do, and they develop more and more anxiety. Let me tell you about a hockey player who learned to overcome debilitating anxiety to become a key player in the success of his team.

Case Study: Winning from Within

> *"Whether I fail or succeed shall be no man's doing but my own. I am the force; I can clear any obstacle before me or I can be lost in the maze. My choice; my responsibility; win or lose, only I hold the key to my destiny."*
>
> **ELAINE MAXWELL,** consultant, coach, and trainer

IN 2011, GOALIE Cam Lanigan took part in a Calgary Flames development camp. Although the camp was the highlight of his career to that point, he felt almost deadlocked after being there.

He found himself unable to get back to top form, and his game took a downward turn that became a spiral. It seemed that he had lost his game, and he fell into a deep funk.

Cam was picked up by the Kamloops Blazers CHL team. After 16 games with them, his statistics were 3-9-0 (wins, losses, and ties) and 0.843 save percentage rate (the top goalies in his league at the time all had 0.9 and higher)—numbers he was desperate to improve. As this performance level continued through the season, Cam was full of self-criticism and constantly faced disappointment on the ice. Because of his anxiety, he almost gave up. Jacques Plante, one of the most important innovators in hockey, knows from experience how tough it can feel to be a hockey goalie. He says: "Goaltending is a normal job, sure. How would you like it in your job if every time you made a small mistake, a red light went on over your desk and 15,000 people stood up and yelled at you?"[1]

What Cam did next was remarkable, and it revealed true strength of character and true grit. Instead of giving up, he took responsibility for getting back on track, back to his best self. With the help and support of his parents; his dedicated and focused goalie coach, Dan De Palma; and me, his brain trainer, Cam put together a plan to get better. Cam decided to enlist us to support him as a personal performance team. The state of his mind was high on his list of priorities, and Cam took responsibility for training his brain to create a whole new mindset. He began to develop trust in the advice of his team. He realized that by learning the most efficient ways to deal with his anxiety, he could face his embarrassment and guilt. Cam

Turn that mean chattering monkey into a ninja monkey that will help you find your inner strength.

and I worked together so that he could learn to retrain his brain, and we formulated a strategy that would see his self-esteem rise. On the ice, the results began to show.

After three months of one-on-one confidence training, Cam brought his mental game to a level where he finally felt free of self-criticism and disappointment on the ice. He was able to simply play—and play well. But the most rewarding part of our work together was the happiness he was able to reestablish within himself. Everyone around him noticed.

On the road to the Memorial Cup that year, Cam was a surprising key player in the tumultuous contest that is lovingly known in Kamloops Blazers country as "Game 6." The night of the game, the atmosphere in Kamloops' Interior Savings Centre was charged to the hilt. As I write this, my arms still tingle with the memory of the greatest hockey comeback I've ever seen. In that unbelievably emotional game, Cam found his feet, his confidence, and his self-control—as well as ways to increase his save percentage. We saw him step up, gather this mental strength, face his fiercest competitors, and, with his teammates, make magic happen.

The whole team stood strong, stood proud, and raised their game to a new level. They pulled back the series from three down to take the Portland Winterhawks to Game 7. That night, I wasn't the only person who was shouting Cam's name and shedding tears of pride for the hard-won success of all those young hockey players on the ice. Teammate Austin Madaisky praised Cam in a post-game radio interview: "Lanny stood tall all game." As Cam's parents wrote in a powerful letter that I reread often, "The Old Cam has come back!"

All the hard work that Cam had put into developing his performance paid off. He was transferred to the Medicine Hat Tigers, where he was repeatedly named CHL player of the week and took his save percentage to 0.960 the following season. Then Cam was invited to try out for the Detroit Red Wings.

Now I'm going to tell you some of the tricks, tips, and mind hacks that I trained Cam to use to help himself. He used these and the tools in the rest of this book to get past his crisis, to deal with his anxiety, to move into a place of personal best, and to step into the confident mindset that legends are made of.

Ninja Monkey Pokes Back

"Nothing can stop the man with the right mental attitude from achieving his goal; nothing can help the man with the wrong mental attitude."

THOMAS JEFFERSON, American founding father and third president

LET'S GET BACK to that chattering monkey of the mind that causes mayhem to our confidence and makes us doubt ourselves. Every day, your thoughts present you with opportunities to feel anxious, and as a player, you may often experience anxiety and worry about your hockey ability. Maybe things didn't go right at practice and you feel frustrated. Perhaps someone on the other team got lippy with you, and their words are still ringing in your ears. Perhaps the team owner came to watch practice but didn't see you playing at your best.

Often we can feel powerless to control our anxiety. I am going to show you how to take back the power and use the anxiety to your advantage. I'm going to show you how to turn that mean chattering monkey into a ninja monkey that will help you find your inner strength. The key is to be aware of what goes on in your mind when you are anxious. When you are aware of what's going on, you can *deal* with what's going on. You can face this challenge that many hockey players come up against regularly—and overcome it.

Anxiety is a (sometimes painful) poke from the chattering monkey of the mind to make us aware that our focus is on what we *don't* want. Did you know that we can learn to use anxiety to help us train our brains to refocus on successful results? Do you remember learning about monitoring your self-talk in Chapter 1? The mind doesn't pay much attention to the *do* or *do not* part. The more you tell yourself not to think about chocolate, the more you want it.

So if a hockey player is anxious about his performance, guess what his mind will be focusing on. Yep, poor performance. Gold medal Olympian Henrik Lundqvist knows a thing or two about developing a strong mind. The only goaltender to record 30 wins in each of his seven NHL seasons, Henrik says, "Things can go wrong at any time. I know that, but it's stupid to focus on the negative."[2]

Sometimes we may feel as though we're thinking a thousand thoughts a minute. But did you know that the mind can actually handle and process only one thought at a time? When our minds are racing, each thought is being presented on the movie screen of our brains for just a moment, and then we move on to the next thought. With awareness of what's happening, we can learn to control what we see playing out in the movie of our minds. We can refocus our mental energy.

Montreal Canadiens star goaltender Carey Price has talked about developing his mindset during the run to the gold medal at the 2014 Olympic Games in Sochi. He could have focused on the fear of losing his position as starting goalie for Team Canada. Instead, he chose to concentrate on something far

---

It takes time and practice to learn something new and then to master that new skill.

---

more powerful. "I wasn't focused on that train of thought, that mindset," Price said when he was asked whether he had felt the starter's job was his to lose. "I was just focusing on what I've done all season and just got prepared to stop pucks. It worked out."[3] It worked out very well. Carey got a shutout and Team Canada got the gold.

So we can use anxiety as a tool to train our brain to focus on getting better results. When we realize that we are feeling anxious, we become aware that our thoughts are causing that anxiety. We can then begin to see that our focus is on something that we fear. When we recognize what's happening with our thoughts, we are being given an opportunity to use those feelings of discomfort as feedback. We then get the chance to actively change our focus to a new, more powerful perspective. Over time, this refocusing of our thoughts helps us to actively strengthen our mind by developing faith in our own ability.

Often the first sign that my thoughts are not correctly focused is when I realize that I feel uncomfortable or uneasy, or my breathing becomes tighter. As soon as I realize that's happening, I know I have allowed my mind to wander to thoughts of worry and anxiety. So I listen to my gut, pay attention to my breath, monitor my thoughts, and change my internal focus and perspective. I use those physical signals to tune in to and evaluate my thoughts, and if I need to, change my thinking.

If you have a game coming up and you are feeling uneasy, notice what your mind has been focusing on. Ask yourself whether you're focusing on your fear of failure or developing faith in your own ability. Use this awareness as a trigger to refocus on a positive outcome.

Give yourself time to practice this refocusing technique. Do it every single time an anxious thought comes up. It will take repetition—every new habit does. We know that it takes time and practice to learn something new and then to master that new skill. This time, you will be training your "mind muscles." Use this mental training as a tool to give you that edge over your competitors. In the words of Reggie Crist, Olympic alpine skier and pioneer of ski cross, "It's amazing how much of this is mental. Everybody's in good shape. Everybody has good equipment. When it really boils down to it, it's who wants it the most and who is the most confident."[4]

Feeding Your Mind

"Champions aren't made in gyms. Champions are made from something they have deep inside them. The will must be stronger than the skill."

MUHAMMAD ALI, legendary boxer and activist

DOES IT EVER seem that you're chasing the puck but never quite catching up to it? Remember Wayne Gretzky's famous quote: "A good hockey player plays where the puck is. A great hockey player plays where the puck is going to be."[5] How can you get to be a great hockey player? By feeding your mind daily to develop your mental performance to create trust and faith in your own ability. You can do this by monitoring the quality of the words you use.

Did you know there is a nutrient quality to every word you choose to use, just as there is a nutrient quality to every mouthful of food you eat? The taste of a fresh piece of fruit, a bowl of delicious homemade chicken noodle soup, or a delectable treat from the local bakery affects the body in many ways. Food can make us feel good and provides energy, comfort, and an opportunity to recharge. In a similar way, the words we choose to use affect how we feel—that is, if we are aware of the power of those words.

Negative words have low energy and increase anxiety. Positive and inspiring words are far more nutrient rich, and they replenish your mental and emotional reserves. The words we use, both in our minds and when we speak out loud, are

WHAT WE THINK AND SAY CAN ACTUALLY CHANGE THINGS WITHIN US, NOT ONLY EMOTIONALLY BUT ALSO PHYSICALLY.

concentrated focusers of energy and nutrition for the mind. Good words focus good energy; they feel good to say. Low-esteem words focus low-esteem energy; they sound hollow and make us feel anxious. By speaking positively to yourself and to others, you can feed your own positive mental energy and develop your powerful confidence.

Your thoughts and words influence the person you are and who you will become. Retired Calgary Flames player Gino Cavallini was talking to a young fan about the important connection between the quality of what we think or say and the quality of who we become. He said, "When you think or speak badly about yourself, you become it, but when you think or speak positively about yourself, you become it too."[6]

Think well, speak well, and be well. All too often, we talk to ourselves in a way that isn't positive. The words we choose to use, to ourselves and to others, have an impact on our ability to be successful in both hockey and in life.

Do these words sound familiar?

· How could I be so stupid?
· Why did I get that shot wrong?
· Why did I do so badly?
· What is wrong with me?

How do you feel when you say those words to yourself? Worried, uncomfortable, anxious? The words we use internally and externally may be able to affect us even more than we realize.

In 1999, Japanese researcher Masaru Emoto studied how thoughts and feelings can affect physical reality. Emoto experimented with the effect, both written and spoken, of different words on water molecules. After freezing the water, he found that the ice crystals were brilliant and colorful when positive words had been directed at the water, and dull and ugly when negative words had been used.

How can we use the findings of a Japanese visionary to help us play better? Our bodies are 70 percent water. Emoto's

---

Take the time today
to feed yourself each hour
with a positive form
of verbal nourishment.

---

findings suggest that what we think and say can actually change things within us, not only emotionally but also physically. Our communication with ourselves and with others has consequences. Our words have an impact on both our internal state and external performance.

The mind hears and stores negative words. If they are heard enough times, the words can start producing anxious behaviors within us as if those negative statements were absolutely true. For example, I convinced myself when I was a child that I was no good at public speaking. For years, I told myself that I was *awful, awful, awful at speaking in front of people*...

So guess what happened? When I stood up to speak, I would develop incredible anxiety. I felt bad, I hated the way the words sounded in my ears, and I looked frightened. That behavior, that frightened response to having to speak in public, was all based on my negative self-talk.

Now before I stand up to speak, I say out loud the positive outcome that I expect. I take the time to picture myself sharing my experiences, connecting with and helping the audience members. That helps me feel good, and the words, when they come, sound powerful and purposeful. It's amazing how your perspective can change when you are mindful of the words you use and change your self-talk accordingly.

Think well, speak well, and be well.

From now on, be diligent when choosing your thoughts and words. Your communication with yourself and with others influences your mind so profoundly that you can sabotage your chances of success. Use your words and self-talk to supercharge your results. Here are some examples:

- What did I learn from that challenge?
- What was good about how I took that shot?
- What was successful about that practice?
- What did I do better this time than I have ever done before?
- What did I get right?

Now you know that words have wings, and you know the power of words, so speak good things. It is vital that you start to become aware of what you are saying to yourself. What you focus on grows. One negative word can lead to using many, many more, either to yourself, in your own headspace, or when speaking with others. Even in jest, nutritionally poor words can affect our physiology and the way we feel about ourselves. A putdown heard too many times can start to ring true, whether it comes from inside us or from someone else. A positive word to yourself or to others can nourish a life, fill a heart, develop a profound and powerful self-esteem, and change the outcome of a game. It can ignite your personal power. Words full of warmth and sincerity can fill you up to the brim with pride and happiness.

Take the time today to feed yourself each hour with a positive form of verbal nourishment. A good word goes a long way. You may find that you're addressing a hunger that lies within. The impact this will have on your hockey will nourish you more than you know. Nurture your body with the finest foods, and nurture your mind with the most powerful thoughts. In the words of poet Ralph Waldo Emerson, "What lies behind us and what lies before us are small matters compared to what lies within us."[7]

Tips

1. Notice when that mean monkey of the mind is chattering away and refocus your thoughts into a ninja monkey that will help you find your inner strengths.

2. Use anxiety to train your brain to refocus on what it is you *do* want.

3. Act and speak out of faith that you have the ability to learn how to deal with any situation.

4. Your thoughts and words influence the quality of the person you will become, so monitor the quality of the words you use.

5. Use positive self-talk to increase your mental energy and nurture your deepest desires.

THREE

SUPERCHARGE YOUR SELF-ESTEEM

Opinions: Yours and Theirs

"Your time is limited, so don't waste it living someone else's life. Don't be trapped by dogma—which is living with the results of other people's thinking. Don't let the noise of others' opinions drown out your own inner voice. And most important, have the courage to follow your heart and intuition. They somehow already know what you truly want to become. Everything else is secondary."

STEVE JOBS, co-founder of Apple

WE'VE ALL BEEN there, haven't we? We feel good about who we are and what we do, we're smiling, laughing, and happy, we feel like we're on top of the world . . . and then, with just a few negative words from another player, a family member, or maybe even a coach, we crash right down to earth.

What happens when you feel like someone doesn't like you? A whole team of players may like you, but if there's one who doesn't, does it become your whole focus, sapping energy out of you like a slow leak in a balloon? Let me tell you, worrying about who likes you and who doesn't is just like juggling tigers. That worry can be hard to handle. The anxiety builds up and can become an uncontrollable animal.

Worrying about people liking you and throwing zoo animals around is senseless and draining. It's not empowering or constructive, and it destroys your focus. When we try to please everyone all the time, we run the risk of wasting energy trying to please the wrong people. We leave ourselves drained of mental energy. We question ourselves, we second-guess ourselves; we self-sabotage and our self-esteem gets pulverized.

Have you ever met someone and felt awesome, just by being in their company? Maybe it's a great friend who laughs at your jokes, who enjoys playing hockey as much as you do. This person is easy to get along with. They get you. You can see they're happy to see you in their face when they smile at you.

And have you ever met someone you felt you just couldn't enjoy being around? Someone you couldn't get through to? Someone just so very different from you that being around them feels like hard work? Perhaps they look mean, or they say negative comments about their family, or their teammates.

Some people react by thinking, *I have to get this person to like me.* This longing to be liked is very natural. Who wouldn't want to have other people enjoy their company? Getting everyone to like you might be a big challenge for you. In trying to get everyone to like you, you might be wasting valuable time and energy… energy that would be better used to focus on and achieve your real dreams and goals.

It's important to understand that there are going to be people who are hard to get along with, and that's okay; that's life. There are some foods that we don't like to eat, some art that we don't enjoy, some tunes that we don't listen to. That's okay; that's life. Do we waste our time listening to music that we don't like so that eventually we might learn to like it? No, we don't. So is it worth trying again and again to get that one person to like you?

We can do something far more rewarding instead. Think about the top 10 people around you who have your best interests at heart. This might be your agent, your coaches, your family. Focus on spending your time with them, instead of the person who is hard to get along with. Listen to their opinion, give their opinion your respect, and when their opinion differs from yours, know that they are offering you a different point of view, one that is worth at least considering.

It is worth taking the time to ask questions to develop your understanding of the trusted person's point of view. All too often, we make assumptions about other people's opinions. The tricky part about assuming motive or intention is that we will never be able to see the world through the eyes of another person. Miguel Ruiz, a truly inspirational writer, spells out our need to take the time to ask questions and understand what people really mean when we hear them speak. "Don't Make Assumptions," he says. "Find the courage to ask questions and to express what you really want. Communicate with others as clearly as you can to avoid misunderstandings, sadness and drama. With just this one agreement, you can completely transform your life."[1]

Hall of Famer Scott Niedermayer learned to do this when his New Jersey Devils coach Jacques Lemaire was trying to teach him to play better defensively. "I thought I knew everything then, but I didn't. I learned a lot and I'm thankful for it. I can tell my younger self that now."[2] Under Lemaire,

Niedermayer and the Devils won a Stanley Cup. Taking the time to understand different points of view and build better relationships with your friends, teammates, coaches, and family will also positively affect your self-esteem.

But it can be hard to listen to the opinions of others, especially when it's the opinion of your coach and you don't like what they say... or even how they say it. One athlete I trained had to deal with criticism from her coach. A coach so tough that his words were weakening her self-esteem. This brilliant young lady asked me to train her brain with mental performance techniques to deal with the criticism and turn it into a way of fueling her success. The training helped propel her straight to the Olympics.

Case Study: Olympic Success

"Success breeds success."

MIA HAMM, two-time Olympic gold medalist and
FIFA Women's World Cup winner

HAVE YOU EVER felt criticized? Was that person someone you felt was judging you? Would you have felt a whole lot better if you knew this person was trying to help you? If you answered yes to any of these questions, you are not alone. In fact, you have something in common with a great athlete.

Elli Terwiel was fighting for a place on the Canadian national ski team. Again and again, she had to deal with the terrors of serious bodily injury to claw her way toward the top. The one thing that was harming her mental attitude was the judgment of one of her coaches. She knew the coach was trying to find ways to get her to ski faster and closer to the edge. What she struggled with was the *way* he spoke to her. The tone and the words he used seemed harsh, unjust, and unfair. Maybe you know how that feels, too. Time and time again, Elli tried to shrug off the words of her coach, yet they still bugged her. They bugged her so much that her skiing was affected and she was worried that she was never going to be picked for the national team.

Worrying about who likes you and who doesn't is just like juggling tigers.

Elli says, "I was training in Saalfelden just before going to my last World Cup in the Czech Republic. I was struggling a little with my times and changing my skiing to adapt to the hill. I was having a hard time processing the coach's critique and turning it into positive goals to work toward on the hill. My lack of trust in myself, my equipment, and the snow to really take risks going down the slope led to slow times in comparison to

The tricky part
about assuming
motive or inten-
tion is that we
will never be able
to see the world
through the eyes
of another person.

the other girls, and the coaches were not finding the right way to help me get over this lack of trust and self-sabotage.

"In training sessions with Izzy we focused on a very specific technique. We focused very specifically on my successes. In skiing you really have to make a conscious decision to 'let go' and take the risks as they come. Izzy trained me to find a huge number of successes in a two-and-a-half-minute regular training session that I had recently run. She challenged me to find 50 to 60 successes in that tiny space of time! It took a little while, and then I found 5 successes, and then I found 10, and on and on and on. However small, I managed to find real worthy successes.

"During the two and a half minutes, I really focused on the technical things about skiing that I am skilled at . . . how I know my body is incredibly strong, technical cues like being able to really push forward on the tops of my boots and arc into the top of the turn, as well as how my equipment is tailored just to my skiing. I thought about the amazing feeling of surprise and reward I feel when I do have a great run. I focused on that feeling at the top of the course the next day as a way to prepare myself to have a good run. After my sessions with Izzy, I really just allowed myself to have confidence in the outcome and let myself take all the risk necessary to really have a run that was 'on edge.'

"I did find myself having good runs in training after that session, and I skied well in my last World Cup, which was a few days later. I found that reiterating the feeling of having just had a successful run before I did my actual run put me in the right mindset to tap into what makes me fast. I find that this mindset of imagining yourself succeeding before you start a project, a run in gates, etc., has really allowed me to lose my fear of failing. And this lack of fear has made me more available mentally to experiment with things. This has helped me in school, life, and in my skiing."

We can feel crippled by our lack of self-esteem, yet we can change the way we feel.

Elli used this tool to develop such strong self-esteem that when she heard her coach's words, instead of experiencing them as criticism, she tuned in to how these words were giving her the opportunity to learn how to get better. She became able to focus on the ways to improve, rather than the tone and the negative words that the coach used to try to help her. She found ways to reframe the criticism into opportunities to learn, develop, and grow.

This tool to supercharge self-esteem also helped Elli achieve her dream. In 2014, she was chosen to represent her country in Sochi at the 2014 Olympics. By using the technique of finding 50 to 60 successes in a two-and-a-half-minute race,

Elli says she was able to "draw from internal sources of power that I was not fully aware of before. I am now more able to see the opportunity and positivity within situations that I was previously struggling with, and I am now a lot happier in those situations! I was able to work through a blockage in my mindset that was affecting my relationship with my coach and my training."

Here we have a very powerful technique to defend the mind against the onslaught of another person's opinion. Elli knew that the coach who was critical of her was doing his best to help her, yet it was only when she was able to balance her mind with many small successes that she felt able to listen to the teaching in his words and deal evenly with their tone and delivery. The seeds of success are sown daily. Set your mind to sow, germinate, and nurture those seeds—in whatever form they take.

Building the Blocks of Self-Esteem

"Self-esteem is as important to our well-being as legs are to a table. It is essential for physical and mental health and for happiness."
LOUISE HART, author, speaker, and community psychologist

WHEN WE THINK about how we respond to knocks to our self-esteem, often the first early warning sign is physical. We might feel a knot in our stomachs, we might hear our breathing become faster, we might see ourselves playing hockey that's not up to our usual standard. Our Spidey sense, our intuition, is telling us that we are feeling uncomfortable and anxious. We can feel crippled by our lack of self-esteem, yet we *can* change the way we feel. There are other tools to build the blocks of our self-esteem.

First, let's start by noticing how you feel right now. Are you relaxed or tense? If you are not feeling relaxed and confident, how can you unwind, release that tension, and feel better? You can learn to actively relax.

Active relaxation is a powerful tool that I teach hockey players to supercharge self-esteem, deepen confidence, and release physical and mental tension. This step-by-step exercise is straightforward, and relaxation happens naturally as a result of releasing your activated muscles. The technique gets you to engage each muscle in turn and activate it fully. The resulting release of each muscle can be achieved only by releasing muscle tension, so you quickly switch to a state of relaxation. It's a method of powerfully recharging your physical energy, as well as your mental energy, by releasing tension.

Here we go. Starting with the feet, tense all the tiny, medium, and large muscles and hold them tight for at least a whole minute. When you absolutely cannot tense your feet muscles to their full strength any longer, release them and move up the body to your next set of muscles. Make sure you spend time with each and every muscle set within your body, including the muscles in your face.

At the end of the exercise, allow yourself a deep breath in and out to replenish every single cell in each of the muscles you've consciously activated and relaxed.

THE SEEDS OF SUCCESS ARE SOWN DAILY. SET YOUR MIND TO SOW, GERMINATE, AND NURTURE THOSE SEEDS—IN WHATEVER FORM THEY TAKE.

Enjoy the process of active relaxation and use it daily. Just before you go to sleep is a perfect time. It can be used anywhere at anytime. In fact, often my hockey players do it between shifts on the ice. You can use this exercise easily during long periods of travel between competitions, even if you're crossing multiple time zones. It will help you unwind the brain and unwind the body. With repetition, this will become one of the most powerful and simple tools that you'll learn. And with practice, you will become proficient at identifying areas of tension and letting them go. We learn quickly that our ability to identify and release strong negative emotions and physical tension increases our capacity to build self-esteem and increase confidence.

The Hero Within

> *"If you cannot do great things yet, do small things in a great way."*
> **NAPOLEON HILL**, author of *Think and Grow Rich*

IF YOU WANT to be more successful, begin by recognizing the success in each moment, just like Olympic and NHL athletes do. You will be able to deal more easily with your coaches and even your families; after all, they often want only to get the best from you. With a high level of self-esteem, you will see that far more easily.

Let's learn from a hockey player who played for the Vancouver Canucks. Brandon Reid remembers only ever wanting to be a hockey player. One challenge for him was staying confident. He points out that recognizing his successes helped him: "I overcame it by working hard on myself during the off-season, on and off the ice—from working out harder in the gym, to working with a sports psychologist, to continuing to remind myself how I got to where I am and of my past achievements."[3]

Enjoy the process of active relaxation and use it daily.

Do you ever think to yourself, *I will know I'm successful when (this) happens*? Know that your day has already been full of success. List your successes, however small, so far today and stop when you get to 20. This form of positive self-assessment supercharges your self-esteem.

Similarly, if you aren't scoring, take note of the small details in your game that you *are* taking care of. The more you notice and appreciate the smallest successes, the more you will boost your self-esteem, increase your mental energy, and get closer to achieving your goals. Former NHL coach Tom McVie says, "You've got to go to the net if you want to score."[4] Why? Because focusing on and recognizing that you're doing the smaller stuff, like going to the net, will bring even more opportunities and results, like scoring. When you recognize the small important actions you're doing today, hold on to the experience and appreciate it. As you extend your focus on the right moves that you are making, you will become aware of the uplift in your mental energy as your success rate increases. You are strengthening your ability to feel good about the choices that you are making, which is developing a suit of armor to protect your self-esteem. You are developing a more powerful perception of your own value.

Value Your Value

> *"There is overwhelming evidence that the higher the level of self-esteem, the more likely one will be to treat others with respect, kindness, and generosity."*
>
> **NATHANIEL BRANDEN**, self-esteem psychologist

WE LEARNED EARLIER, in Chapters 1 and 2, that words have wings, so speak good things. How we speak to others is often how we speak to ourselves. In fact, the level of value, the level of self-esteem, that we have for ourselves shows in the words we choose to use.

Hall of Famer Steve Yzerman played his entire NHL career with the Detroit Red Wings and is now the general manager for the Tampa Bay Lightning. When Yzerman was honored with the prestigious Order of Hockey in Canada, Bob Nicholson, former head of Hockey Canada and now CEO of the Oilers corporation, said this about him: "You just watch how hard he works, how he communicates to other general managers, and how he communicates to his players."[5]

To supercharge your self-esteem, speak well to and about your family, your team, and your coach; speak well to and about yourself. Anything else sabotages yourself and the results you seek to achieve.

As Mexican author Miguel Ruiz urges, "Be Impeccable With Your Word. Speak with integrity. Say only what you mean. Avoid using the word to speak against yourself or about others."[6] We must be diligent with our thoughts and our words. Even the words we choose to use in our thoughts affect the way we feel. If we are feeling uncomfortable, then we are thinking uncomfortable thoughts. The mind and the body are connected.

As a young defenseman with the Detroit Red Wings, Cory Emmerton deliberately chose thoughts that helped him deal

---

Today, and every day, we need to speak to ourselves with kindness and respect.

---

with being the new guy on the team. He said of his early days, "I told myself to stay positive—at least I was getting the opportunity to play on a good team and play a lot."[7]

Today, and every day, we need to speak to ourselves with kindness and respect. When we do, we increase our self-value and self-esteem. When we *change how we speak* to others and ourselves we can *change how we relate* to others and ourselves. Author Napoleon Hill devised principles for success that are now used worldwide. One of his key success principles was, "Every man is what he is because of the dominating thoughts which he permits to occupy his mind."[8] Hill was describing the power of our thoughts, which trigger us to take action, and it is our actions that trigger our results. By monitoring our thoughts, we are able to have a positive impact on our actions and results.

Start to monitor your thoughts today and carefully choose the subjects that you dwell upon. Even before he was drafted, star defenseman Jay Bouwmeester talked about not dwelling upon negative experiences and thoughts, saying, "If something doesn't go right, you just come back and get it right the next time. You are going to have good nights and bad nights, so you just got to go with it and have fun."[9] Bouwmeester knew that we all deserve to speak well to ourselves, about ourselves, and to others. We all deserve to feel valued by ourselves and by others.

> **"You have to take pride in yourself."**
> PAUL COFFEY

In the words of the Buddha: "You yourself, as much as anybody in the entire universe deserve your love and affection." Once you find one thing that you like about yourself, you start to develop self-esteem and self-appreciation. From the smallest appreciation within us comes an increase in happiness, peace, and success. This is a very powerful action tool.

Who in the hockey world uses this tool to help himself? Hall of Fame defenseman Paul Coffey, one of the all-time leading NHL defensemen. He says, "You have to take pride in yourself."[10] Look for any and every opportunity to appreciate

From the smallest
appreciation
within us comes
an increase in
happiness, peace,
and success.

yourself, your actions, and your ability to play hockey. It may be as simple as thinking, *I can do so much more now on skates than the first time I laced up.* A deep appreciation for the smallest increase in skills encourages the mind to find ways to keep improving.

You deserve to take this step forward every day from now on to supercharge your self-esteem. Today and every day, treat yourself with the respect and appreciation that you deserve.

Tips

1. Take the time to consider the opinions and points of view of those who have your best interests at heart, instead of those you don't get along with. They might offer you a different perspective and help you develop as a player.

2. Ask questions to develop your understanding of the other person's point of view. Use this technique to build better relationships with your friends, teammates, coaches, and family and supercharge your self-esteem.

3. Strengthen your mindset against the onslaught of other people's opinions by becoming aware of your many small successes.

4. A strong mindset, and good self-esteem, can enable you to see opportunity in even the toughest situations.

5. Monitor your self-communication—the way you speak to yourself is the key to your success.

6. Take the time to actively relax daily.

7. We all deserve to feel valued by ourselves and by others. Speak to yourself and others with kindness, appreciation, and respect to increase your self-value and self-esteem.

FOUR

TURN STRESS NIGHTMARES INTO MIRACLES ON THE ICE

Two Players, Same Situation, Different Results

*"I think the greatest amount of pressure is the pressure
I place on myself."*

CATHY FREEMAN, Australian Olympic sprinter

STRESS IS THE mental and emotional tension we experience
when we are put under pressure. It can affect us in many ways.
All too often, I see stress show up on the ice. You might have
seen it too. Stress can show up in our physical bodies—our
heartbeat can get faster, our mouth might get dry, we might get
butterflies in the stomach, twitching, muscle tightness, blush-
ing, pacing, sweaty palms, sleepless nights, nausea, and even
vomiting. Stress can show up in our behavior—nail-picking,
nail-biting, playing it safe, avoiding eye contact, irrational
emotional outbursts, low energy, procrastination, and feeling
"locked up" inside and unable to take action. What happens in
our brain when we are stressed? We get confused; we have bad
focus; we feel rushed; we have poor self-talk; we feel weak, dis-
satisfied, indecisive; and we increase the criticism of ourselves
and others.

Think of the player who freezes under pressure. Analysis
paralysis sets in. He overthinks, and he doesn't know where

to send the puck. Think of the goalie who is slow to react. The burden of being the gatekeeper for his team weighs too heavily on him. He misses the easy saves, and he hangs his head as he comes off the ice. Think of the player who has negative self-talk. You can hear him beat himself up with his words. His focus and attention are purely on the negative side of his game and he's not being fair to himself. He has stressed himself out. Trying to deal with stress can be a nightmare. It can make it hard to even concentrate on the game.

Concentration can be an epic challenge. We have so much to distract us, and technology moves so fast that our minds are constantly switching gears and trying to take in the next concept or idea as fast as possible. We no longer have to be patient in the search for information, products, or ideas, as instant gratification comes to us at lightning speed through our smartphones, tablets, and computers. The way we use our devices is changing how we use our minds. With that change can come loss of focus and dwindling attention spans. Now more than ever it is crucial for hockey players to learn techniques to retrain their brains to deal with stress by increasing their mental focus.

Take two players who are dealing with the same stressful challenges in their hockey. Player number one might be fighting the stress of the problems he faces day to day by wallowing in his horrible luck and complaining about what is lacking in his playing, in his team, and in his coach. This player lacks energy, feels hopeless, and thinks that everything that happens is just another nail in his coffin of suffering and torment.

Now take player number two. Although he faces the same challenges, he looks around and takes stock of what ability he does have and uses it to propel himself forward. He looks at what he *is* able to do and how he has learned from his previous challenges. It might be the ability to skate fast and the determination he has to get better and the belief that by being hardworking and determined, there is always hope and the possibility of change. This second player is resilient and through his resiliency, he expects to find the learning in the challenge and focuses his attention on how to change his game for the better.

What if you could focus your attention so specifically in ways that would change your game for life? You could use this focus to increase your love of the game and radically affect how well you play. Really? Is that possible? It is. One player did just that.

Case Study: An Avalanche of Opportunity

"Everything negative—pressure, challenges—is all an opportunity for me to rise."

KOBE BRYANT, professional basketball player

COLIN SMITH HAS always been a gifted player, a player who lights up the rink when he plays. He is one of the most tenacious players I've had the pleasure of working with. What struck me when I first met him was his sheer determination

Now more than ever it is crucial for hockey players to learn techniques to retrain their brains to deal with stress by increasing their mental focus.

to improve his game by becoming mentally stronger, even if it meant that we worked together every single day. His goal was clear: to play in the NHL.

Colin faced similar challenges to his teammates. He had to deal with the highs and the lows of his sport. He had to learn his hockey skills; he had to deal with his coach's opinions; he had to cope with the press, both good and bad; he had to manage the long, long bus trips; and he had to do all this while being far from home. Colin was also one of the smaller players on his team—he had a whole lot to prove. Yet what was different about Colin was that he actively sought to develop his brain as much as his physical ability. He knew that dealing with his stress nightmares was the way to develop his game, though would it be enough to achieve his dream of playing in the NHL?

Colin learned that our reactions to everything that happens, big or small, determine what actions we take, how we feel about ourselves, and ultimately, what results we achieve. Every thought, action, and reaction has the incredible power to make or break us, so making the new habit to concentrate in the right way is an invaluable skill. Colin proved that with determination to change, practice, repetition, and focus, this skill can be learned.

I trained him to review his daily experience in a way that powered up his mental attitude. Colin learned to retrain his brain by sweating the small stuff—in a good way. People can be powerfully negative in their thoughts about their lives and experiences. Add debilitating, destructive fear, and we might be hard-pressed to remember our own name. We know that negative thoughts lead to negative actions, whereas positive thoughts lead to positive actions. Positive thoughts set the scene for opportunities for us to learn and grow and develop. Positive thoughts open us up to learning from each experience and using that learning to understand what we need to do to get better. In the words of Tiger Woods: "A lot of people look at the negative things, the things that they did wrong and—which I do. But I like to stress on the things I did right, because there are certain things that I like to look at from a positive stand-point that are just positive reinforcement."[1]

That first season, I set Colin the task of powering up his mindset by emailing me three successes, however small, from his day that made him feel good—every day. Colin learned to fuel up his mental energy and set himself up with an expectation that he would learn from the experiences of the next day, just as he had today. This established a very powerful positive feedback loop.

Colin found that his focus on what he had done right set him up to deal well with his stresses on and off the ice. The stress nightmares became manageable and beatable as he began to see them as opportunities to learn. He used these challenges to develop his game.

Fast-forward to today and Colin still emails me every single day and lists three successes from his day. Colin has become so good at defining the strengths of his day that this technique has enabled him to find the opportunity to see the miracles in every single day. Even when he is not playing hockey, Colin now nat-urally focuses on the good outcomes of the day, no matter how challenging. He is learning from living.

What about Colin's dream of playing in the NHL? Well, he didn't get drafted to the NHL, and his friends did. In response, Colin rolled up his sleeves and got back on the ice and back to work training his brain. His hard work and dedication paid off. Colin has now played for the NHL team the Colorado Avalanche. He realized not being selected the previous year had helped him, saying, "Getting picked by Colorado was a huge honor, but I think it was important for me to have learned the summer before when I didn't get picked."

We can all develop our emotional tools daily by focusing on the opportunity to learn from our actions and experiences. We can all learn new skills every day like Colin. We can all use this tool to turn our stress nightmares into miracles.

Fearing and Failing

"To be a champion, you have to learn to handle stress and pressure. But if you've prepared mentally and physically, you don't have to worry."

HARVEY MACKAY, businessman

FOR ALL OF us, our attitude to learning life's lessons can be summed up in one of two ways. Are we acting from fear of the outcome or faith in our ability to deal with the possible outcome? The problem with operating out of fear is that we're on shaky ground. The outcome we feared might not have happened anyway! We are acting from a place of low self-esteem and perceived low ability to cope with the outcome. All too often, the choices we make from this position do not help us get the results we desire. For example, if we choose to avoid the next practice after a tough hockey game because we fear that we are going to play badly in the next game, then we are avoiding the opportunity to practice, train, improve, and learn to be a better, stronger, more capable player. We are not operating from a place of confidence and courage. We are afraid of what may happen.

However, we *can* choose to focus on our hockey abilities and have faith that whatever happens, we will find a way to get better. In the same example, another player, with a determination to be stronger and better, would *choose* to focus on how that tough game showed him areas of his play that he needs to work on and learn from the feedback and experience. He would look for that opportunity to improve in the next game. The key here is to pay attention to your thoughts to see whether you are acting out of fear or faith.

After joining the Pittsburgh Penguins as the number one pick in the NHL draft, Sidney Crosby was stepping into a whole new world, and he knew that he had a lot to learn. He said, "I'm trying to learn as much as I can out there, but I'm confident in what I *can* do."[2] He chose to be confident and act out of faith in his own ability. He focused on what he *could* do. We all do some things well and some things less well. We just need to find a way to make each experience count.

Failure does not make or break us. What is important is how we choose to react to failure.

POSITIVE THOUGHTS SET THE SCENE FOR OPPORTUNITIES FOR US TO LEARN AND GROW AND DEVELOP.

Wayne Gretzky said, "You miss 100 percent of the shots you don't take."[3] He didn't stop shooting at the net because he missed a shot. Instead, he learned from those shots and kept going. We too can choose to use our challenges as ways to learn what we need to do so that we can get better. When we stumble and fall, which we all do, it is an opportunity to discover what we need to do next time to succeed.

Catching Curve Balls

"You can't control the curve balls life throws you, so you have to learn how to control yourself and change quickly to make sure the curve ball doesn't knock you out."

MARK EDWARDS, media innovator

ONE OF THE athletes that I train is a member of the United States national development baseball team. In baseball, a curve ball is a pitch thrown with a strong downward spin. The ball drops suddenly and veers to the side as it gets closer to the plate. In hockey, and in life, a curve ball is the term we use to describe something that is unexpected, out of the blue, and often disruptive. An example of a curve ball for a hockey player might be that he's suddenly traded to another team, or benched for half the season, or injured. The most common curve balls in hockey are injuries. NHL Hall of Famer Brad Park often had to deal with curve balls he didn't see coming, including hits to the face. "We get nose jobs all the time in the NHL, and we don't even have to go to the hospital!"[4] says Brad.

How do we deal with curve balls? When the world throws us a curve ball, it is presenting us with an opportunity to learn—about ourselves, our situation, or maybe even both. Curve balls are eye-openers. The truth is, we all have to deal with events and situations we didn't plan for, like, in Brad's case, facial injury. In my experience, and in training others, I've seen that time and again, when the world throws us a curve ball, we get the opportunity to learn, grow, and develop. We then realize that curve ball was exactly what we needed to learn how to catch. In the long run, curve balls often provide us with what we needed to learn in order to win the game.

Sean "Puff Daddy" Combs says, "Everyone has challenges and lessons to learn—we wouldn't be who we are without them."[5] We all have the ability to be dragged down by the ebb and flow of everyday life. Some days are outstanding; other days, the challenges and obstacles can make our hearts sink to the floor. We all also have the ability to learn from the ebb and flow to propel us on our next journey. After all, there was once a time when you couldn't read a letter, let alone a sentence, yet here you are, reading the words written on this page.

Star hockey players Jim Craig, Tony Amonte, Keith Tkachuk, Rick DiPietro, and Chris Drury have all played for the Boston University Terriers, but there's only one jersey hanging from the rafters in their arena—Travis Roy's. Eleven seconds into Roy's first shift, he was checked into the boards and became paralyzed. After the shock of his injury had begun to subside, Travis chose to make the best of his very tough situation. He chose to deal with the curve ball that life had thrown at him. He refocused, regrouped, and created a great future by making the most of his present. Travis earned his degree, started the Travis Roy Foundation dedicated to enhancing the lives of spinal cord injury victims and families, and has contin-ued to make every day count.

Every single day in our lives, we face down obstacles and curve balls. We have to in order to develop and evolve. It's what we do naturally. The key is to stay focused on our goals and learn from the challenges we face. Superstar defenseman and Hall of Famer Ray Bourque summed it up well: "Be relentless in pursuit of your goals, especially in the face of obstacles."[6]

Finding Perspective

"Injury in general teaches you to appreciate every moment. I've had my share of injuries throughout my career. It's humbling. It gives you perspective. No matter how many times I've been hurt, I've learned from that injury and come back even more humble."

TROY POLAMALU, NFL player

THERE ARE TIMES when we feel overwhelmed by challenges. In sport, we are used to the emotional roller coaster, peaks and troughs, busy times and crazy busy times. We have days when we wish that time would stand still to give us a break from the craziness we find ourselves in. Then come the quiet days, when we draw our breath and do whatever we can to recharge and get ready for the next onslaught. Sometimes we feel like we are being pulled in many directions. We can become stressed, tired, mentally and physically exhausted, and unable to connect with the peace of mind we all deserve to have on a daily basis. Stress can affect how well we play hockey. It can be hard for us to maintain a balanced perspective. As George Eliot wrote in *Middlemarch*, "It is a narrow mind which cannot look at a subject from various points of view."

Although we cannot control the curve balls life throws at us, we can change how we react to them. We can choose to change our perspective. We can choose to take a step back from the situation to perceive it differently.

Failure does not make or break us. What is important is how we choose to react to failure.

There is a mental performance training technique that my players use to change their perspective on a tough challenge. They start by imagining that they are in a movie theatre, watching themselves trying to deal with the challenge in the movie that is taking place on the screen in front of them. They are watching themselves and the whole situation from a new perspective, the perspective of an outside observer. Their mind gets to see the situation more clearly and from different points of view—the perspective of each actor on the screen, as well as the viewer. I train them to use this tool to develop the habit of taking a step back to get a clearer view, a wider perspective, to deal with a stressful situation.

If they want to supercharge this technique and get an even more powerful perspective of the situation, I train them to imagine they're up in the projector room of the movie theatre, watching themselves sitting in the seat down below, watching themselves and the situation unfold on the screen. This is called "double dissociation" and gives them another shift in perspective, another step back from the emotional charge of the situation. They get to see the whole situation play out as if they are their own head coach. Looking at the big picture helps them see new opportunities, discover new solutions, and turn their stress nightmares into feedback to develop their game.

When Pittsburgh Penguins center Brandon Sutter was asked to switch from his usual position to play right wing with Sidney Crosby, he chose to use this change as an opportunity to develop his game. "I think it's just a little bit of a different way to look at the game, different perspective of it," he said.[7] He saw the opportunity in playing on the team's top line.

Taking a step back allows you to change your perspective and find new solutions to the challenges you face. Different points of view can often help you find solutions you never would have seen otherwise, solutions to help you achieve your goals and build your ability to play creatively and create miracles on ice.

Tips

1. Two players, same situation, different results. Your mindset makes the difference.

2. Focus on the good, however small, until it becomes the great.

3. Pay attention to your thoughts. Act from faith in your own ability to deal with a situation instead of from fear of the possible outcome.

4. Know that we naturally learn and grow and develop, each and every day.

5. Choose to learn today so that you can face down obstacles tomorrow.

6. When the world throws you a curve ball, change your perspective and use it as an opportunity to learn how to catch.

FIVE

SELF-BELIEF STALLING? GET IT BACK IN GEAR

Becoming the Person You Were Meant to Be

*"You've got to go out on a limb sometimes because that's
where the fruit is."*

WILL ROGERS, humorist

SELF-BELIEF IS THE confidence you have in yourself and your
own ability. Self-belief is the spur that prods you to be creative
and courageous with your hockey. Self-belief allows you to
take risks, take chances, stand out in a crowd. It inspires you
to raise your game, it helps you deal with tough opponents, it
enables you to learn from feedback and feel good about your
progress and your success. When your self-belief stalls, your
state of mind, your happiness, and your hockey can be deeply
and negatively affected.

Stalled self-belief can make us feel deeply uncomfortable. When we feel anxious and overwhelmed, we can feel
off balance and unstable. This can make us feel like we're
being pulled in many directions. We can become stressed,
mentally and physically exhausted, and unable to connect
with the peace of mind we all deserve to have on a daily basis.
We feel ungrounded. We question ourselves. We might even

self-sabotage and find ourselves crippled by a feeling of nausea caused by our lack of self-confidence. This lack of self-belief can affect how well we play hockey, especially if we feel overwhelmed by the many other demands on our time.

As athletes, we participate actively in life. Sometimes we are so focused on our sport, we find ourselves nervous, tense, tight, and unable to get into "the zone," where our game flows naturally. We may feel like our emotions are going up and down. Although we cannot totally command this peak and trough cycle, we can change how we react to having way more on our plate at one time than we want.

How do we do that? When we take care of the basics, we build a strong foundation on which success can grow.

Case Study: Coming Back from the Brink

ONE OF THE hockey players that I trained had a life that was 100 percent about hockey. In his words: "Everything else was secondary. I would bury everything I didn't like or want to deal with deep inside myself and try to forget it. When hockey didn't go as well as I wanted, I felt like everything I had done up until that point in my life was a waste. I was filled with anger, frustration, and worst of all, regret. As well, all the emotions I had buried within myself came back. I was a wreck." When we began working together, goalie James Leonard felt that his self-belief was at an all-time low.

Working together, we were able to see through the mess of stalled self-belief. James dug deep and learned to use tools to remind him of the person he really was deep down. We cleared the roadblocks to self-belief, giving him the ability to regain the confidence, the composure, and the level-headed state of mind needed to be successful in every aspect of life, not just hockey. Not only did his motivation to become better at hockey improve, but his desire to become a greater human was also fired up. Things that were not as important as hockey before seemed more important now, allowing him to relax, live in the moment, and enjoy hockey more. He says, "I now know how to deal with negative impacts on my life better than I ever thought possible."

Self-belief is the spur that prods you to be creative and courageous with your hockey.

By training his brain, and developing his self-belief, James Leonard changed his life for the better. He became more grounded, balanced, and focused, and was awarded the Kootenay International Junior Hockey League's (KIJHL) Conference Player of the Month. He was designated the regular season and play-off MVP, and the Kootenay Conference Eddie Mountain

Division goalie of the year. In James's words: "It truly was a great year on and off the ice!" The improvements that led to his success started with developing his breath health.

Grounding Yourself, Checking Your Breath Health, and Feeling the Flow

"I make sure I always surround myself with good, down to earth, fun, real people, who always keep me grounded."
SEAN KINGSTON, rapper

WHEN YOU FEEL wound up tight like a spring, check your breath. Are your breaths short and fast? If they are, I bet your thoughts have become fast and furious too. Then, check your self-belief. There's a good chance that's stalling, too.

Here's what you need to do to get right back on track. Check your "breath health" regularly throughout the day. Your state of breath reflects your state of mind. Are you breathing calm, smooth breaths at times when you feel it's appropriate to do so? Do you feel capable, grounded, and balanced? If not, read on.

The mind and body are deeply connected; the state of one is reflected in the other. The following technique supercharges your mind/body connection. It takes you to a place of peace and quiet, reminiscent of the sounds you would have heard in the womb and a replication of the calm, restful sounds you hear near the ocean. With a calm state of mind, your self-belief can get back into gear.

Start by slowly inhaling and exhaling through your nose. Close your windpipe enough as you do this to make a hissing sound. If you sound like Darth Vader, you're doing it right!

As you listen to the gentle noise in your windpipe, you are regulating the flow of breath in and out of your lungs. Rather than using your lungs like bellows, you are using your windpipe like a hose and moderating the flow of air in and out of your body. Focus on making sure your breathing is smooth, easy, effortless, calm, and relaxed. Within minutes, you will start to feel more physically and mentally relaxed.

This technique is called Ujjayi breathing—though one of my clients, Canadian pro snowboarder Marlie Marchewka, calls this her yogi breath. This breathing method regulates your airflow and rebalances your emotional state. Do this before a game or competition, or even before a tough conversation with your coach. Then, just as you realize you are tensing up, use the yogi breath to become calm and focused once more.

When you feel wound up tight like a spring, check your breath.

Practice this for a total of 10 minutes at first, once a day for one week. Pay attention to how long it takes until you are breathing easier and feeling better. With practice, you will be able to shift your comfort level and get yourself back into gear, just by monitoring your breath health. Eventually, you will be able to attain almost immediately a state of relaxation and flow, while consciously making a mind/body connection that serves you well at the time when you need it most.

THE MIND AND BODY ARE DEEPLY CONNECTED; THE STATE OF ONE IS REFLECTED IN THE OTHER.

There is another breathing technique that develops your mind/body connection, as well as your ability to create a calm internal environment.

Learning to Exhale

"I'd like to be a more consistent starter. I'd like a smoother transition from crouching to running. I have to learn to relax during a race and how to breathe."
DONOVAN BAILEY, Canadian Olympic sprinter

THERE IS AN Indian saying, "We are all given a certain number of breaths in this world, and we are meant to use each one wisely. The worrisome mosquito is in a rush and uses all of his up quickly in a life that lasts a few hours. The elephant is wise in her use of each of her breaths and lives well for a very long time."

We can mimic the wise elephant and use our breath another way to ground us and remind us how confident we feel when we are balanced and grounded.

Here's how to learn to exhale. For every breath you take in for the next 10 minutes, breathe out for twice as long as you breathe in. Use your breath to calm down and feel like you're in the moment. Being in the moment means being focused on the here and now. It means not worrying about past or future events. When we are able to be mindful and present, we are able to fully experience this moment in time and reset our inner awareness. We get to have a mental time out. As you become more observant, and notice the small differences that make all the difference, you will be able to observe the physical and mental shifts that happen almost immediately.

Being Present

> "*The power for creating a better future is contained in the present moment: You create a good future by creating a good present.*"
>
> **ECKHART TOLLE**, author of *The Power of Now*

BEING PRESENT AND being mindful allow us to become very attentive to what is happening in the moment. And this affects our ability to have focus and confidence. This next technique powerfully and positively affects our ability to play our game at speed and have the perspective needed to deal with blows to our self-belief quickly and effectively.

Buffalo Sabres left winger Matt Ellis shares what he did to deal with the challenge of being sent to the Sabres' farm team. He could have seen this as a demotion, but instead, he says, "When I was sent to Rochester last year, [I told myself] my role has changed, my team has changed, focus on the day, where I'm at, focus on the present."[1]

So how do you become present? By building on the last technique, once your breathing is calm, and you feel grounded and secure, the next step starts right here. Begin by focusing your attention completely on exactly what it is you are doing right in this moment. Hold that attention for 10 seconds. Ask yourself, what do you notice, right here in this moment? What can you see, smell, hear, taste, and feel? Right here, right now, all is good. You are present. When you are able to be present for at least 10 seconds, double the length of time until you can be present for the duration of a whole hockey game.

The most powerful players and most successful athletes that I have worked with have mastered the art of being present. This training in breath work and self-control can help you develop a mindset and a focus that bolsters your self-belief and becomes one of your greatest assets.

Listing Your Assets

"You are your greatest asset. Put your time, effort, and money into training, grooming, and encouraging your greatest asset."

TOM HOPKINS, America's number one salesman

HERE'S ANOTHER TECHNIQUE for strengthening self-belief. When you get caught up in thinking about the things you feel you cannot do, its time to put your achievements into perspective. Remember, there once was a time when you could not hold a book, read a page, or write your own name. Your list of achievement is lengthy, and it is only natural that this list will grow longer today.

In your mind, list three skills that you have developed since you first set foot on the ice. Then decide what you will achieve today to add to your list.

Star NHLer Ryan Walter has good advice for those tough days when your self-belief is stalling: "Persevere. Stay dedicated and keep pursuing!"[2] Walter played more than 1,000 games with the Washington Capitals, Montreal Canadiens, and Vancouver Canucks before coaching and working for the Calgary Flames. He knows a thing or two about staying grounded during the ups and downs of hockey. He does it by being mindful of his assets and achievements to develop his self-belief and hockey confidence.

What's So Special about You?

"Praise you like I should."

FATBOY SLIM, DJ, musician, and record producer

HALL OF FAME goaltender Bernie Parent shared some advice on how to develop our ability to feel good and believe in ourselves. He said, "Be kind, engaging, share compliments, care. Be the one to brighten someone's day, make someone else smile. You will make others feel good about themselves, and you'll be surprised how good you will feel in return."[3]

Positive reinforcement is the key to encouraging great behavior. Guess what? What works for other players around you, works just as powerfully for the person inside of you. Take the time to praise yourself for your good qualities—for turning up to practice, for helping your linemates score, for reading about the game, and for being determined to train your own brain. When you take the time to make yourself feel good for doing good, more good will follow. Self-talk has a huge impact on your self-belief, which in turn affects your performance. Self-talk can also directly affect your perceived level of luck.

Luck Is Yours for the Taking

"I've found that luck is quite predictable. If you want more luck, take more chances. Be more active. Show up more often."

BRIAN TRACY, success expert

A DAY WHEN you feel lucky can feel like the best day of your life. You feel supercharged in your self-belief and in your ability to accomplish goals easily. Everything is going your way. On the flip side, a day when you feel that everything is going against you, when your self-belief evaporates, when simple tasks feel impossible, can feel like the unluckiest day in the world.

So are you lucky or unlucky? Well, it depends on how you frame your experiences. Either way, you will ultimately find what you seek. "You make your own luck," says Anaheim Ducks coach Paul MacLean. "If you work hard enough and you play hard enough, things can go your way. Obviously we're playing harder, and that's what makes puck luck."[4] Hard work brings good fortune, and a mind that looks to find that good fortune will be luckier than most.

"Today I can complain because the weather is rainy, or I can be thankful that the grass is getting watered for free." This anonymous quote is an example of a simple reframe of a situation to make the best of it. A reframe is a filter through which we can choose to find opportunities instead of limitations in each situation that we face.

When you take the time to make yourself feel good for doing good, more good will follow.

In 2013, Milan Lucic entered the play-offs coming off a disappointing regular season. The Boston Bruins star recognized the chance to turn the entire season around, though, saying, "I saw it as an opportunity to get my game back to where I wanted it to be and show that I am still able to be a big-game type of player."[5]

Lucic reframed his challenge in order to find the good luck in it. We can too. We can use this method to find good

We can reframe
and train
our brains to
identify more
opportunities for
health, happiness,
success, and luck
in our game.

luck and to shift our self-belief back into gear. We can choose now and each day to reframe and train our brains to identify more opportunities for health, happiness, success, and luck in our game.

Who and What You Are Matter

> *"There is vitality, a life force, an energy, a quickening, that is translated through you into action, and because there is only one of you in all time, this expression is unique."*
>
> **MARTHA GRAHAM**, dancer and choreographer

WAYNE GRETZKY WAS known for his ability to see the game unfold; Bobby Orr knew how to make his defensive position offensive; Patrick Roy knew how to perfect the butterfly style of goaltending; Sidney Crosby and pro hockey player Colin Smith know how to make the most out of every ounce of their ability. Successful players make the most out of what comes naturally to them. Being unique is a quality that comes naturally to you, and you can use your unique qualities to get your self-belief back into gear.

Here's how: Take the time today to ask someone you love and trust for three positive words they would use to describe you and your game. Listen carefully to their positive responses and focus on your unique qualities until they feel good. Then use those good feelings that come from that great feedback to build your self-belief.

This tool to develop your self-belief will lead you to receive a compliment from a person you trust and respect. Do you ever feel shy or self-conscious when someone gives you a compliment? Author and motivational speaker Leo Buscaglia said, "Too often we underestimate the power of a touch, a smile, a kind word, a listening ear, an honest compliment, or the smallest act of caring, all of which have the potential to turn a life around."[6] Gifts come in many forms—a compliment is a verbal gift.

Use your unique qualities to get your self-belief back into gear.

It can be tough to accept the verbal gift offered to you. Hockey superstar Wayne Gretzky says, "The highest compliment that you can pay me is to say that I work hard every day, that I never dog it."[7] When we are paid a compliment, it's important to show our gratitude for the verbal gift that we have been given. If you don't know quite what to say, just quietly say thank you, breathe, acknowledge your good luck that someone thinks well of you, and gently accept the gift you have received. Finally, use that good energy to help build your self-belief.

Tips

1. Monitor and maintain your breath health to build a strong foundation on which success can grow.

2. Use your breath to ground you and help you feel the flow.

3. Being present, mindful, and positive affects your focus and confidence.

4. List assets and achievements to develop self-belief and hockey confidence. Reframe challenges to find opportunity in each and every situation.

5. Learn to give and take praise and gracefully accept a compliment to feel good about your unique qualities that make you successful.

SIX

SHARPEN YOUR FOCUS AND RAISE YOUR GAME

Manage Expectations, Supercharge Results

"Don't lower your expectations to meet your performance. Raise your level of performance to meet your expectations. Expect the best of yourself, and then do what is necessary to make it a reality."

RALPH MARSTON, the Daily Motivator

HOW CAN WHAT we choose to focus on affect our game? If we expect the best in life, we will find it. If we expect the worst in life—guess what happens? We find it. Our brain gives us examples of what we are specifically looking for. We find what we expect to find.

A hundred people can look at one hockey game and will have a hundred different takes on that same game. As we learned in Chapter 5, in hockey you make your own luck—it all depends on the expectations we have set in advance of the situation.

When I was young, my mum would find ways to get me to focus my mind during long bus journeys. We would play the red car game. We had to shout out when we saw a red car on our journey. The winner was the person who saw the most red cars.

I remember thinking that when we played that game, there seemed to be far more red cars than we would regularly see. The same thing happened when we switched the game to how many blue cars we could see. Out of nowhere, there seemed to be more blue cars on the road than usual. What was going on here? Well, the number of red or blue cars hadn't changed, but our choice to pay attention to them had. We were focusing our minds to find a specific result.

Now, how can we use this childhood game to manage our expectations and supercharge our results?

We know that what we focus on grows. In the case of the red car game, paying attention to the potential for seeing red cars means we do actually *notice* more of them, even though the number hasn't increased. So if we want a positive outcome from each experience we have in life, we have to actively start looking for, and expect to see, the positive in each situation we face.

Here's a mental performance technique to sharpen our focus by raising our expectations. Start each day with the intention of taking three of the day's experiences, good or bad, and in each situation asking, "What have I learned here that will enable me to become a stronger and more powerful and successful hockey player?"

When we choose what to take from a situation ahead of time, we are training our brains to notice and be prepared to act on opportunity. We are setting ourselves up for success. We are developing our ability to be more flexible and choose how to respond positively to the challenges we face on a daily basis.

The most powerful and successful people we know are often experts at staying calm and grounded in the most challenging situations. They are preprogrammed to look for the most effective way of learning and growing from the challenges they face. There is something special to be found in the darkest of days if you are convinced that you are going to find it.

While working with the Hockey is for Everyone program with Willie O'Ree, Gerald Coleman, a player of color, shared that he had been actively discouraged from playing hockey because of the color of his skin. He was told that he would never make it as a hockey player. He responded by making the most of every opportunity he had to play the game that he loved. He resolved: "I'm going to be a goalie, and I'm going to play in the National Hockey League."[1] Coleman focused on his goal, he managed his powerful and positive expectations, even in the face of other people's negative expectations, and it paid off. He supercharged his results. He played with the Tampa Bay Lightning and is still in professional hockey as a goaltender. His circumstances fueled his determination to find light in the darkness of other people's opinion. We can learn from his determined state of mind.

In hockey you make your own luck.

When Barry Melrose was hired as coach of the Los Angeles Kings, he set his expectations high. "I was coming off two championship teams in three years, so I expected to win every year as the coach, and that's the attitude I went in with when I came to L.A. From day one we talked about winning

I'VE LEARNED THAT THE BEST THING IS TO FOCUS ON THE TEAM YOU PLAY FOR AND YOURSELF AND WHAT YOU NEED TO DO.

SIDNEY CROSBY

the Stanley Cup. I'm a big believer that if you're scared to talk about the Stanley Cup, you're never going to win it."[2]

With practice, we, too, can become this flexible with our greatest asset—our own mind. We, too, can train our minds to focus and expect success. We can decide, right now, what type of positive experience we want to find in this day, in every challenge we face. We then find that others start to be inspired to do the same.

Inspiration: The Key to Your Success

"What matters is to live in the present, live now, for every moment is now. It is your thoughts and acts of the moment that create your future. The outline of your future path already exists, for you created its pattern."

SAI BABA, guru and philanthropist

INSPIRATION CAN BE summed up simply as the process of being mentally stimulated to do or feel something, especially something creative. Great players inspire us, great results encourage us, yet, above all, it is how we use our own mind that most motivates us to get great results. We can be, with our own thoughts and focus, our best inspiration. Pittsburgh Penguins superstar Sidney Crosby has said, "For me, I've learned that the best thing is to focus on the team you play for and yourself and what you need to do."[3] Crosby takes responsibility for his focus, which affects his confidence, his self-control, and his results. As a leader, Crosby knows the importance of focusing on the positive inside us to bring the most out of ourselves.

What about making the most of the inspiration that exists outside of our own mind?

Who inspires you? Who do you see play and think, *One day I'd like to play that well*? Other people, such as players, coaches, and family members, can be powerful sources of inspiration and the key to your success. As peace activist Rachel Corrie said, "We should be inspired by people... who show that human beings can be kind, brave, generous, beautiful, and strong—even in the most difficult circumstances."[4]

Here's how to be inspired by others: Focus on the conversations around you. Listen to your coaches, your agent; listen to your competitors; listen to the people who have what you want and are deeply, truly happy. Listen to the people who have what you want and model what they do and how they do it. What are they doing and saying that you can add to your own life to strengthen your own powerful and positive destiny? Who is speaking words that inspire you to be greater than you have ever been? When you see others achieve the goals that you long to achieve, smile and know that if you take the step to learn from them, you are using your brain in a very smart way to develop your ability to achieve your own goals.

Whether it's playing or coaching hockey, the NHL is often the ultimate goal for young aspiring players. After coaching Nazem Kadri in the Toronto Maple Leafs farm system, Dallas Eakins saw his young pupil enjoy success as a rookie in the NHL. Eakins, former head coach of the Edmonton Oilers, had this to say about Kadri: "Knowing the kid like I do, I'm happy for his success and I'm just glad he's a full-time NHL player right now."[5] The key is to focus on the opportunity to learn from how other people get to be successful. Use the successes of your teammates and even your competitors to inspire you to grow as a player. In her speech at the 2012 Democratic National Convention, Michelle Obama talked about the lessons she and the president had learned from their families.

Use the successes of your teammates and even your competitors to inspire you to grow as a player.

She said, "We learned about gratitude and humility—that so many people had a hand in our success, from the teachers who inspired us to the janitors who kept our school clean ... and we were taught to value everyone's contribution and treat everyone with respect."[6]

Your very first intention and action upon opening this book was to use it for your self-development. Your skill and ability to train your own brain have developed in response to the actions that you have taken over the previous chapters. You are learning to develop your focus and your hockey perspective. One of the most powerful ways to keep training your brain to become more focused and more powerful is to spend time with other people who brighten up your day.

Edmonton Oilers alternate captain Andrew Ference recognizes the importance of being in a positive atmosphere, and being surrounded by inspiring players, even in the NHL. He says, "It wasn't a pressure-cooker situation where guys were gripping their sticks, it was a positive atmosphere where it didn't matter if you were a guy like (Mark) Recchi or a kid like (Tyler) Seguin coming in, everybody was allowed to be themselves and contribute and speak up in the room."[7]

To develop your hockey confidence, sharpen your focus by spending time with people who see the world from a brighter, more positive perspective and value your opinion and contribution. Use that inspiration to raise your game.

Visualization Supercharged

"Visualize this thing that you want, see it, feel it, and believe in it. Make your mental blue print, and begin to build."
ROBERT COLLIER, self-help author

VISUALIZATION IS USED in all sports to give the mind a clear, focused picture of the desired outcome. Pittsburgh Penguins all-star James Neal uses visualization on the ice. He explains, "When you get the puck, you know exactly where you want to

Spend time with
people who
see the world
from a brighter,
more positive
perspective and
value your opinion
and contribution.

put it. You do it before the game, too. I try to visualize all different kinds of shots, angles, you name it."[8]

However, visualizing the outcome you desire using only images is as useful as playing a game of hockey with only one other player on your team. You can be somewhat effective and perhaps achieve your goal, but there is a way to supercharge this tool to be far more effective in helping you focus and get the results you desire. This mental performance technique helps you raise your game by being more intensive, more multidimensional with your visualizations. You can use all your senses to make your visualizations far more powerful and meaningful.

Case Study: Soaring High and Landing Solid

"It comes down to something really simple: Can I visualize myself playing those scenes? If that happens, then I know that I will probably end up doing it."

JESSICA LANGE, award-winning actress

ONE PROFESSIONAL FREESTYLE skier that I work with had a dream. Brett Dawley's burning desire was to finally, after five years of attempting the same dangerous trick day after day, land a switch 540.

The switch 540 is one of the most sought-after tricks for professional competitive freestyle skiers. Taking off backwards, at speed, over huge jumps, to land facing in the opposite direction is a challenge in itself. When you add the total number of spins—a 360 rotation, plus an extra 180 rotation—you can start to imagine the sort of challenge Brett was facing.

Brett's struggle was that his brain would get in his way. He wanted to stay balanced and composed during his switch 540, and he wanted to attack the trick with speed, confidence, and safety. He could see the jump taking place in his head as he tried to visualize his successful outcome, but he didn't have a clear enough mental image to land the jump.

To help Brett, we worked together to make two major additions to his visualizations before he again attempted this potentially dangerous and definitely challenging trick on his skis.

We supercharged his visualization by taking 20 minutes for him to add his other senses to the picture he had in his mind's eye. Brett imagined what he would see *and* what he would hear, feel, taste, and smell when he had successfully achieved his outcome and landed a balanced, safe switch 540 at the perfect speed. He was imagining the feeling he would get when he landed his trick, the smell of the snow, the cheering of the crowds, and the taste of the success. Brett and I worked together to develop his mental preparation. We were giving his mind a far clearer and more powerful prescription for accomplishing his goal.

On top of this we added one more powerful layer to the visualization. I trained Brett to visualize with all his senses the trick not from the start to the finish but second by second by second, from the successful finish to the successful start. We ran the movie image, with all the added sensory impressions, back and forth, back and forth, and back and forth, again and again, until his mind was fully comfortable, happy, and prepared for the move he had been trying to make for the last five years.

Here's what Brett said: "I have now conquered major goals that I have been working on for the past five years and now have more confidence in my big mountain skiing as well." The week that Brett and I worked together on this trick, he successfully landed his switch 540 five times, safely, powerfully, and at just the right speed. And he did this by supercharging his visualization to sharpen his focus, raise his game, and change his results.

Tips

1. Raise your expectations and expect the best to sharpen your focus.

2. There is something special to be found in the darkest moments, if you look hard enough to find it.

3. With practice you can develop mental flexibility.

4. Inspiration comes in many forms. Look for it both in yourself and in the people around you.

5. Supercharge your visualizations to enhance your focus and accelerate your results.

SEVEN

OVERCOME MENTAL ROADBLOCKS TO WIN FROM WITHIN

Protect Your Greatest Asset

"It is better to conquer yourself than to win a thousand battles. Then the victory is yours."
BUDDHA

HAVE YOU EVER had one of those days when anxiety and doubt made you feel sick to your stomach? Have you ever found yourself running around, trying to do your best so that your coach, your family, your team, and most of all you can feel proud of your accomplishments, and then it hits you like a steam train—there's nothing left for you to give.

Do you know how it feels to be completely exhausted? It all gets to be too much, and it feels like it's hard to get through the day. You might wake up at night in a cold sweat, you might hear yourself breathing quickly, and you can't see a way out. If you've been in this position, then you're not the only one. I have too.

I had a huge wake-up call. Right at the time I needed it, right at the time when work and life and the concept of balance were mere passing acquaintances—it happened. I was flying from one city to another, working hard, trying to make sure that I was giving my very best to every person that needed my help. I was exhausted. I had nothing left in the tank. And then, at the beginning of the flight . . . the penny dropped. I tuned in and listened to the words of the cabin crew with fresh ears. As I listened to the preflight safety instructions, I heard, "In the event of decompression, an oxygen mask will automatically appear in front of you. To start the flow of oxygen, pull the mask towards you. Place it firmly over your nose and mouth, secure the elastic band behind your head, and breathe normally."

Here's the bit that shifted my thinking that day: "If you are traveling with a child or someone who requires assistance, secure your mask on first, and then assist the other person."

I realized that for me to be a better brain trainer, partner, athlete, and daughter, it was important that I take care of my greatest asset, my mental energy, and "put my own oxygen mask on first." I finally understood that for me to be around for a long, long time, able to care for and help others, I had to take full responsibility for my own well-being.

That day, I started to put my own basic needs first, tend to them, and then, from a position of health, rest, and strength, I was better able to help those around me. I became a better brain trainer, and a much happier and more successful person. I took time out to help a friend in need. That friend was me.

When we get exhausted, opportunities to take better care of ourselves will become available to us. The trick is to take life by the hand and lead it firmly and gently to a place where you can breathe normally. If you're traveling this life with a hockey team or player or family member who requires assistance, secure your breath first, and then assist the other person.

**TAKE LIFE BY
THE HAND AND
LEAD IT FIRMLY
AND GENTLY
TO A PLACE
WHERE YOU
CAN BREATHE
NORMALLY.**

Put your basic needs first so that you can protect your best asset, your own mental health and happiness, so that you can develop the best game of your life. To become a game changer means that we can shift our results for ourselves and for our team. Often the best game changers in life are the ones who have worked the hardest to take care of themselves so that they overcome mental roadblocks that once held them back from reaching their potential and win from within.

Case Study: Game Changer

> *"You have to learn the rules of the game. And then you have to play better than anyone else."*
>
> **ALBERT EINSTEIN**, Nobel Prize–winning physicist and founder of the theory of relativity

ONE OF THE most powerful athletes that I have worked with is Emma Whitman. She is an inspiration to me for taking the steps needed to overcome her mental roadblocks and change her game. We worked together to regain her mental performance after injury, injury that happened time and time and time again. Over and over, this world-class skier could have given up. Emma questioned her ability to make the right decision—whether to compete or retire. Ultimately, the choice was hers, but she was of two minds about it—part of her feeling confused and the other part wanting to win, so she put all her energy into developing her mental strength.

We transformed her thinking by working together to understand and resolve the conflict between the two parts of her. Just as when two friends need help resolving an argument, we treated each part as if it was a separate person with very specific needs. We identified the purpose of each part's desire and found that both sides wanted to feel safe, secure, and accomplished. Together, we were able to resolve that inner conflict and she felt clear, focused, and relieved. Consistency and safety were the keys to Emma's success.

Develop inner strength, inner focus, inner smile, and inner energy to overcome mental roadblocks and win from within.

Emma's dedication to developing a world-class mindset led to progress and results. Her transformation was nothing short of miraculous. Her headspace had never been stronger. Emma went on to compete and win the Aspen Open. Twice. The following are examples of some of the tools we used to develop inner strength, inner focus, inner smile, and inner energy to overcome her mental roadblocks and win from within.

Inner Judgment

> *"Depend upon yourself. Make your judgment trustworthy by trusting it. You can develop good judgment as you do the muscles of your body—by judicious, daily exercise."*
> **GRANTLAND RICE**, sportswriter

UNTIL WE HAVE walked a mile in another person's shoes, how can we really know what they have experienced? If we don't know exactly what another person is dealing with inside their mind... how can anyone else really know what's going on in ours? Calgary Flames star Theo Fleury was a player who was judged by others. "My whole life, people told me I couldn't accomplish much," he shared,[1] adding that he believed he was capable of proving them wrong.

However unfairly we feel judged by others, ultimately, the final judgment of our behavior, thoughts, actions, or skill is ours. If at the end of the day we can truly say we have done the best we could, then our inner judgment must reflect how hard we worked, how much we helped our team, how much more we want to learn tomorrow. Our judgment of ourselves can be as harsh or as rewarding as judgment from others. Harsh self-judgment leads to mental overload and roadblocks that prevent us from winning.

Do you judge yourself harshly or fairly? Are you appreciating the miracle of your life or taking your skills for granted? Are you appreciating the skill you have at this moment as a reader, or maybe the ability you have to use tiny muscles to turn over a page in this book? Jack Canfield, coauthor of the Chicken Soup for the Soul series, says, "By taking the time to stop and appreciate who you are and what you've achieved—and perhaps learned through a few mistakes, stumbles and losses—you actually can enhance everything about you. Self-acknowledgment and appreciation are what give you the insights and awareness to move forward toward higher goals and accomplishments."[2]

Harsh self-judgment leads to mental overload and roadblocks that prevent us from winning.

Vladimir Konstantinov of the Detroit Red Wings was already one of the best defensemen in the NHL, finishing second to Brian Leetch for the Norris Trophy, when devastating brain trauma from a car accident ended his career. He wouldn't have been able to move on to make acclaimed works of art without an ability to focus on and appreciate what he was able to do in this moment.

When reflecting on returning to the NHL after leaving it for the Russian KHL, New Jersey Devils superstar Jaromir Jagr said, "You appreciate things after you lose them. I feel that's probably the biggest difference. I'm excited about every game now."[3] This self-appreciation is an important tool. The words "thank you" are some of the most powerful we can use. We can choose today to find many, many ways to feel thankful and appreciative for what we have and who we are right now. To develop your inner judgment, appreciate more what you have right now, in *this* moment, and choose to be thankful.

Pat Quinn was a tough, excellent stay-at-home defenseman during his NHL playing days, and he went on to become one of the NHL coaches with the most wins of all time. He once told Toronto Maple Leafs tough guy Tie Domi, "Tie, I know you're

Strength is as strength does.

a tough guy and a fighter—if you learn how to play and show me you can play hockey, then you can stay on the Toronto team."[4] Domi made the most out of the opportunity that Quinn had given him, honed his abilities, and then used what he had learned to help others become better. He appreciated his own skills and used them to improve himself and inspire others. Where some players would have seen Pat's words as an ultimatum, or a harsh judgment, Domi chose to take the opportunity to prove himself.

Take the time at the end of each day to be firm and honest with yourself. What did you do well today? What will you do better tomorrow? And always, always know that who you are tomorrow is a new person, capable of learning to be stronger, faster, and fitter. Choose today to judge yourself fairly, acknowledge your success, and show deep gratitude for the skills that you have learned in this lifetime, and then put them to good use developing your inner strength.

Inner Strength

"When we meet real tragedy in life, we can react in two ways—either by losing hope and falling into self-destructive habits, or by using the challenge to find our inner strength."

DALAI LAMA, the spiritual head of Tibetan Buddhism

OUR INNER STRENGTH is a reflection of our peace of mind, and it shines through in our words, thoughts, progress, and actions. Strength is as strength does.

As the first black player in the NHL, Willie O'Ree developed his inner strength to win from within. NHL commissioner Gary Bettman says, "He has a resolve and an inner strength that allows him to do what he believes and not let anything get in his way."

A calm, strong mind is good for our mental and physical health; it's also a major factor in the mental performance of many NHL hockey players. So how do we develop that inner calm that leads to inner strength?

Many of us can relate to actor Tristan Wilds from *The Wire* when he says, "Sometimes I wish that I could go into a time machine right now and just look at myself and say, 'Calm down. Things are going to be fine. Things are going to be all great. Just relax.'"[5] Being calm and alert under pressure is a sign of inner strength. It's the desired and optimum activation level for many athletes. The more relaxed we are, the more our inner strength develops, and the more powerful we become. Dale Hunter was known for his highly spirited play during his 19 seasons in the NHL. Now, as a coach, he shares the importance of remaining calm: "I've taken bits and pieces from all the coaches I've had. And one of the things I liked in a coach was a guy who could stay composed."[6]

A technique for developing a calm and alert state of mind is to take a long-term perspective of the challenge. Taking the time to look at a challenge over a longer period of time opens your mind to new ways of seeing solutions. Ask yourself, will this challenge today mean as much to me in a year from now? And what is this challenge teaching me so that I can grow now to be a better player and a better person?

Mike Babcock is the head coach of the Toronto Maple Leafs, and he coached the Canadian men's Olympic hockey team to gold in 2014. He knows success depends on being relaxed and alert. His technique is to "breathe, just play. We have to get back to playing and we talk about this a lot over the years. We've had tough stretches every year that I've been here and as much as you have to work real hard and compete real hard, it's still not work hockey; it's play hockey."[7] Inner strength enables us to get back on track and focus on winning. Hockey is a game where we have to strengthen our minds to deal with challenges.

The words "thank you" are some of the most powerful we can use.

Mental Strength: A Position of Power

"I developed a mechanism so that whatever mistakes I made, I would bounce straight back. Whatever was happening off the pitch, I could put it to one side and maintain my form. Call it mental resilience or a strong mind."

GARY NEVILLE, English football coach

THE POWER OF being in a positive atmosphere with a grounded and balanced internal emotional and mental state affects our ability to play our best. When we are strong mentally, we are able to develop our hockey confidence. It does take practice; it does take determination. So does hockey.

Valeri Nichushkin now plays for the Dallas Stars, yet in the draft picks, he was passed over by nine other teams. Those teams had missed how mentally strong Nichushkin was and how determined he was to play his heart out

"Breathe, just play."

MIKE BABCOCK

for an NHL team. Doug Lidster, an assistant coach at the time, said of Nichushkin, "I think his skill level is obvious, but there have been other things that maybe the casual observer doesn't see. In our power play walkthrough on the first day, a defenseman lost the puck on a drill. Right away he grabbed another one, threw it back to the guy that fumbled the puck and said in broken English, 'Hey, let's do it again.' He took charge right away. Later on in practice, a defenseman missed a shift and didn't jump out there, so Valeri jumped out and took charge. I like that. I like the fact he's not sitting back despite being in a foreign country, working in a second language and being with a new team. He's jumping out there, trying to become a better player, trying to help his teammates be better. That's what has impressed me."[8]

Lidster has a skill to see beyond the physicality of a player and get an intuitive sense of the mental mettle of the person behind the player. He is a gifted coach who knows the importance of developing mental resilience to power up his players.

Inner Focus

"A man who as a physical being is always turned toward the outside, thinking that his happiness lies outside him, finally turns inward and discovers that the source is within him."

SØREN KIERKEGAARD, Danish philosopher

SITUATIONS CHANGE DAILY. What we experience today we will never get to experience in the same way again. We can choose to develop our mental performance by tightening our inner focus and finding the time to enjoy the moment as much as possible.

This strategy is never more obvious than at the Olympics. Ex-NHL player, now head coach of the Canadian women's Olympic hockey team and assistant coach of the Chicago Blackhawks Kevin Dineen held an after-practice meeting asking the experienced players for advice for the newer ones. "I think a big part of the message was 'enjoy the moment' and

that's where we're at right now," he said,[9] just before going on
to win the gold medal.

We build our inner focus, and develop our mental strength,
by practicing each day and finding every opportunity we can to
feel good and happy about ourselves, our choices, our actions,
and our results. The key is for us to adore what we do today
while we still get to do it. It feels good to win from within.

Inner Smile

*"Your smile will give you a positive countenance that will
make people feel comfortable around you."*

LES BROWN, motivational speaker

A SMILE ON your face spreads your happiness to the people
around you. And feeling happy will lead to an inner smile,
which is another way to build your self-esteem and confidence
to win from within. It's a smile that will also help you feel more
comfortable within yourself. An inner smile, an appreciation of
the miracle that is your life, is one of the most powerful tools
that a hockey player can have to increase their mental strength
and happiness.

The power of positive reinforcement shows up in hockey
all the time. After the Boston Marathon bombings in 2013, the
Boston Bruins and the Buffalo Sabres played a game dedicated
to showing the importance of focusing on the positive. After
the game, Bruins defenseman Andrew Ference summed it up

by saying, "Everyone wants to give people a positive feeling walking out of the rink."[10]

How can you use this inner smile as a tool to train the brain and win from within? There will be some person or situation that will make you smile today. You can choose to focus and experience the good feeling until it intensifies throughout your whole body and strengthens your neural pathways to happiness. Hold the smile gently for three more seconds than you normally would and enjoy it just that little bit more. This will replenish your inner energy.

Inner Energy

"It's so important to realize that every time you get upset, it drains your emotional energy. Losing your cool makes you tired."

JOYCE MEYER, author and speaker

IF YOU ARE serious about being successful, you need to get serious about keeping your inner energy up. My grandmother lived by the saying "Tidy house, tidy mind." She was right. Our outside space is a projection of our inner space. If our outward space is disorganized, guess how well our brains are working? Often the most calm and restful rooms are the ones that are clean and well organized.

Being well organized means that you are able to give yourself the best advantage when you play. You are prepared, you are ready, and you have good inner energy and personal power. This organized place of calm will help you supercharge your hockey confidence to win from within.

Tips

1. Take care of your basic needs first to better help those around you.

2. Develop your inner judgment by appreciating what you have and who you are right now, in *this* moment, and be thankful.

3. Build inner strength by cultivating a calm and relaxed state of mind.

4. Tighten inner focus by finding the fun in each day.

5. Appreciate yourself and build confidence with an inner smile.

6. To get serious about your performance, get serious about your inner energy and stay organized.

EIGHT

REFUEL YOUR MENTAL ENERGY

How Happiness Builds Mental Energy
and Changes Results

"Scientifically, happiness is a choice. It is a choice about where your single processor brain will devote its finite resources as you process the world."

SHAWN ACHOR, happiness researcher, author, and speaker

MENTAL ENERGY IS the drive and desire we have to complete a task or achieve a goal. When our mental energy is low, we can procrastinate, we can feel tired and drained and subdued, we can feel slow and unresponsive. When our mental energy is high, challenges seem easier to deal with, we feel refueled, ready to take on all that the world throws at us today.

Happiness helps us power up our mental energy to produce powerful results. Positive psychologist Shawn Achor has one of the most popular classes at Harvard University. He has studied the relationship between happiness and success, and he found that success does not always bring happiness. He found that only 10 percent of our long-term happiness is predicted by what is outside of us, and 90 percent of our long-term happiness is directly affected by how our brain processes what is outside of us. This is why we find people on the same team who are positive and love their work, and others who see competitive hockey as drudgery and stress. This is why some people love playing tougher teams, and others cannot stand it. It's empowering for us to realize how much control we actually have over our happiness, and how much we can refuel our mental energy.

Happiness helps us power up our mental energy to produce powerful results.

You might know the player who is so hard on himself that he produces fairly good results yet kicks himself for missing opportunities in a game. He brings down his own mental energy, and his mental attitude toward himself limits his performance. His level of productivity is not as high as it would be if he could focus more on his game and less on how much he beats himself up.

Achor also found that happiness is a work ethic. You have to train your brain to be positive, just like you work out your body. Doing one action a day to train your brain to be lighter, happier, more reactive, and more adaptable will have a huge impact on your hockey confidence—and your hockey performance. Although Achor's work is relatively new, some of the most successful players and coaches knew years ago the value and impact of the power of the mind on getting results.

Case Study: The NHL and Beyond

"Here's to ... the ones who see things differently—because they change things ... they push the human race forward."
STEVE JOBS, co-founder of Apple

GUY CHARRON, NHL player, NHL assistant coach, and now Western Hockey League (WHL) coach, has inspired many to become better hockey players, better human beings, and in one particular case, a better brain trainer. Guy is a rare individual in the world of hockey. He is able to see beyond the stats of a player and trust his intuition to know that the player is often capable of so much more. It was Guy who invited me to first work with hockey players and had the foresight to see that the level of mental performance training that benefited Olympic and World Cup athletes was going to be of great benefit to his hockey team. Guy pioneered a new approach for his team, an approach that paid off. I worked with him to develop the team's confidence by addressing one of the most deep-rooted mental roadblocks of each player on the team. During our time working together, Guy's team accomplished a franchise record-breaking number of wins in a row.

Not only was Guy at the cutting edge of developing the mental performance training of his team, but he has also stayed true to his work ethic of bettering himself each and every day, including his own mental performance. Guy worked with me intensively and to this day uses my first book, *101 Short Steps*, as a practical guide for peace of mind. He tells me that he and his wife, Michele, work together to read a page of the book and take that single action a day that will lift their mental energy to a new level. Guy has seen the game of hockey from all angles, and he knows what it means to be truly committed to becoming better each day. Always improving, always seeking ways to develop his state of happiness (as well as his golf handicap!), Guy's work ethic is exceptional. He is an inspiration to others. He knows the importance of happiness and its impact on our ability to be successful. But he is not the only successful NHL player to develop his ability to be happy.

Hockey Happiness

"I couldn't beat people with my strength; I don't have a hard shot; I'm not the quickest skater in the league. My eyes and my mind have to do most of the work."
WAYNE GRETZKY, hockey legend

AS A KID, Barron Smith, son of the great NHL defenseman Steve Smith, would spend weekends hanging out with his father in NHL locker rooms. "I noticed how all the guys would always come to the rink with a big smile on their face. I figured if I wanted to be happy, I'd play hockey because I like it. I want to come to the rink every day with a big smile on my face."[1]

**YOU HAVE
TO TRAIN YOUR
BRAIN TO BE
POSITIVE,
JUST LIKE YOU
WORK OUT
YOUR BODY.**

Barron noticed at a young age that happiness is something you can work toward. Happiness is the consequence of personal effort. It is a task that one actively participates in. Does anyone tell you happiness is all in the mind? They are right, that's where it starts. So how do we develop our ability to be happy and successful and increase our mental energy to get results?

Taking Care of the Business of You

"If you don't take care of yourself, cater to yourself and that little inner voice, you will really not be very worthy of being with someone else, because you won't be the best version of you."
KIMORA LEE SIMMONS, fashion designer

FEELING HAPPY, ACCEPTED, and appreciated are important needs for us all. Think about it: Do you play better when you feel good about yourself? Me too.

To take care of the business of you, you need to become aware of your basic needs and take care of them. The more conscious you become of what your needs are, the more creative you will become in finding ways to meet them. This will lead to more confidence and more mental energy to develop your game and become more successful on and off the ice. In the words of basketball coach John Wooden, winner of 10 NCAA championships, including a record-holding seven in a row: "Success is peace of mind, which is a direct result of self-satisfaction in knowing you did your best to become the best you are capable of becoming."[2]

Hall of Famer Howie Meeker recognized a huge need early on. He needed to have a long-term goal to work toward. "From the first time I got a pair of skates I wanted to be a pro player," he says.[3] He made a name for himself playing junior hockey;

Happiness is the consequence of personal effort. It is a task that one actively participates in.

---

served in the Second World War, where he would travel to any game he heard about; and then came home and played in the Ontario Hockey Association. Shortly thereafter, he made it to the Toronto Maple Leafs, where he won the Calder Trophy as the league's best rookie. He became aware of his needs and his responsibility to take action and fulfill those needs.

When we take the time to consider what our needs are and find ways to fulfill them, it has a huge impact on our self-esteem and self-belief, refuels our mental energy, and enhances our ability to play superb hockey. Hockey players learn early about the need to stay physically healthy. As Chicago Black-hawks all-star Patrick Kane says, "Take better care of yourself as far as eating and different things like that."[4] But this can be taken further.

"Everything for me is all about self-care," says *Glee* actress Lea Michele, "because I really feel that if I'm at my best, then I'm able to come to my job and really be feeling the best."[5]

Your level of self-care influences your level of mental energy. One of the best ways to increase your confidence and happiness and get great results is to take responsibility for your self-care. Each time you take good care of yourself, you improve your state of mind, and this has a positive impact on how well you play hockey.

Curt Fraser learned the necessity of self-care after finding out he had diabetes. "It actually might have helped me because I had to focus on really taking good care of myself," he says. "I had always been into physical fitness, but after I found out I was diabetic, I took even better care of myself."[6] He went on to play more than 700 games in the NHL and is currently assistant coach with the Dallas Stars, helping many more players.

You can choose today to create a stronger, happier, and more successful state of mind by taking excellent care of yourself to refuel your mental energy. Your need for self-care is as strong as your need to be taken care of when you were first born. The difference is that now you can provide that care for yourself. Perhaps one of your needs is to have a lighter, happier, more upbeat mind that deals well with challenges. (Me too.) So how do we unblock those mental drains that can negatively

The more
conscious you
become of what
your needs are,
the more creative
you will become
in finding ways to
meet them.

affect our ability to be happy? We learn to better manage our mental energy.

Managing Your Mental Energy

"You can train your mental strength just like you train your body. If your body looks fit or ripped, it looks strong, and you can flex your muscles. So, physically, you have certain strength. Mentally, it's the same thing. You can train your psychological strength."

WLADIMIR KLITSCHKO, professional boxer

DO YOU EVER have those days when you feel mentally drained? Was it easy to play hockey that day? Very often we let ourselves experience the negative energy and the effects of the ebb and flow of the day and feel drained. This can leave us feeling powerless and out of control.

Do you ever have those days when you feel that you got so much done that you could have kept going on forever and ever? Was it easy to play hockey on that day? Would you like to have more of the high-energy days than the completely drained ones? You can.

When you drive a powerful car, you can monitor how much of the fuel you are using throughout the day. Likewise, when you learn to pay attention to how you use your mental energy, you can decide when and how it is to be used. You can also make pit stops to refuel.

Over the next seven days, list 10 things that drain your energy during the day. To identify energy drains simply look at a situation or conversation and ask, "Has this made my mood higher or lower, brighter or darker? Is my mind more or less energized?" Events or exchanges that lower your mood are energy drains. Typical examples include:

· Talking to people who bring down your mood.
· Eating food that makes you feel unhealthy.
· Feeling guilty for not being fully committed during your last game.
· Reading negative news reports.
· Watching violent TV shows or the news.
· Replaying your lost game over and over in your mind.
· Reviewing feedback from your coach.
· Receiving criticism from family members or teammates.
· Reviewing how well you slept last night.
· Thinking about how your last media interview went.

We have all been there. It doesn't look great, it doesn't sound great, and it doesn't feel great. So what can we do?

The trick is to train your brain to find 10 ways every day to actively refuel your mental energy.

Typical examples could be:

· Watching your favorite hockey player on YouTube for 20 minutes.
· Sitting in the sunshine.
· Talking to your favorite positive person.
· Practicing your stickhandling skills.
· Exercising.
· Listening to a hockey hypnosis recording.

- Remembering the very first time you met your partner.
- Seeing the joy on the faces of your team when you won your last game.
- Reviewing great feedback from your coach.
- Watching your favorite TV shows.

Taking responsibility for your personal mental energy will put you in a position of confidence and control over your life.

When I trained a client of mine to do this, she found that she no longer got pulled into long drawn-out conversations about how dismal and difficult life is. She was attracted instead to connecting with people who daily looked for the best in people and in life, even if they were going through mentally draining situations of their own. She started to surround herself with more and more opportunities to learn from challenges,

---

Letting our joy and our passion for our game show brings its own rewards.

---

and it was easier for her to have more mental energy. With that learning to become a stronger, more balanced, and energy-conscious person, she found it easy to move forward quickly toward achieving her goals. She took responsibility for her mental energy levels and made it a priority to refuel and recharge. Her abilities to have self-control, take care of herself, and take care of business became far more powerful. So how do we attract more mental energy?

Increasing Your Mental Energy

"When you are enthusiastic about what you do, you feel this positive energy. It's very simple."
PAULO COELHO, author

DOING WHAT WE love is very attractive. It lifts up our spirits. Our eyes sparkle, we are happy about life, our joy is infectious. It attracts people to us. We get noticed by scouts, management, agents. In hockey, having great mental energy attracts new opportunities. Letting our joy and our passion for our game show brings its own rewards.

Hall of Fame superstar Wayne Gretzky's eyes sparkle when he speaks about his love for his sport. He says, "Listen, everything I have in my life is because of the NHL and because of hockey, and I love the game and I loved every minute of being a player, I loved coaching, I loved being involved in the NHL."[7]

We can follow Gretzky's lead and increase our mental energy by focusing on our love for the game and letting that enjoyment shine through our actions and play on the ice. Another way of attracting great mental energy is to pay the good vibe forward to help others.

Paying It Forward

*"Help others achieve their dreams and you
will achieve yours."*
LES BROWN, motivational speaker

THEY SAY NO man is an island. One of the single most powerful attitudes and states of mind that I have seen in the greatest
hockey players is the ability to help others. Whether it's taking
the time to help another player practice and develop his skills

---

Paying goodwill forward is an easy way to develop your mental energy.

---

or remembering a billet mom at Christmas with the gift of a
phone call, investing some of your time in helping others will
always be paid back—sometimes in the most unexpected ways.
Where we get to in life is directly correlated to whom we help
and support and how good that makes us feel. It can feel good
to say thank you, and that good feeling increases our mental
energy. Paying goodwill forward is an easy way to develop
your mental energy. The key is to make sure that you only pay

goodwill forward when you are in a happy and successful state of mind.

Tips

1. Happiness is something you can work toward to refuel your mental energy and produce powerful results.

2. Create a stronger, happier, and more successful state of mind by taking excellent care of yourself.

3. Identify energy drains and find ways every day to refuel your mental energy.

4. Increase your mental energy by focusing on your love for the game.

5. Paying goodwill forward is an easy way to develop your mental energy.

NINE

FOLLOW YOUR OWN TRUE NORTH

Standing Strong, Staying True, Setting Your Own Course

"Don't try to be somebody you're not because it doesn't work. If you try to be this perfect person or perfect persona of what you think that somebody should be, it's just not going to work. Just be yourself, stay true to your core values."

BEN QUAYLE, American politician

HAVE YOU EVER had a coach or a boss scream and shout at you? Ever had a colleague or training partner give up long before the game is lost? Ever had a person act irrationally toward you? If the answer to any of these questions is yes, you are not alone. When it comes to success in hockey and in life, standing strong in the face of the outbursts of others will enhance your ability to maintain composure and control on and off the ice.

Sometimes other people's behavior and opinions may be a shock. Every person you meet is doing the best they can with the resources they have available to them. Here's the challenge for them—they are not you and can never be you. They can only present you with an opinion of you, filtered through their own eyes and their own experience.

Know that each person you meet is doing the very best with the resources they have. In terms of mental resources, studying how a person reacts to you gives you an opportunity to develop a deeper understanding of their beliefs and values. This may be just the insight you need to connect with them so that they feel understood. The key here is to balance their opinion against what you know deep down inside to be true. Ask yourself, are they acting in your best interests, do their values match yours, are they speaking from experience, and are you able to learn from their opinion? Will taking their advice help you become happier, more composed, more self-aware, more content, more successful? Is following their advice setting you up for a journey that's right for you? According to Tabatha Coffey, author of *Own It! Be the Boss of Your Life*: "Sometimes, in order to follow our moral compass and/or our hearts, we have to make unpopular decisions or stand up for what we believe in. It can be difficult and even frightening to go against the grain, whether it's a personal disagreement with a friend, partner, or family member or a professional decision that affects coworkers and colleagues."[1]

The most powerful tattoo I have ever seen is of a compass without any directions labeled on it. The tattoo reminds the wearer, my fiancé, William Dallimore, to always follow his own true north and no one else's. I look at that tattoo every single day, and its advice has always set me up to steer my own ship in the right direction, even when my journey was very different from those around me. We may often feel uncertain of our next step. The key is to take the time to make well-informed decisions so that we can take the steps that make us feel comfortable, strong, and true to ourselves. In the words of Morihei Ueshiba, founder of the martial art aikido: "Everyone has a spirit that can be refined, a body that can be trained in some manner, a suitable path to follow."[2]

In life, in hockey, finding our own true north is essential for accurate navigation in a way that's right for us. Hockey superstar Bobby Orr summed this up beautifully when he was asked what made him keep playing hockey. He said, "I just loved the game, and didn't think of wanting to do anything else. I would do anything to play, if it meant going on the pond or staying late at the rink. I felt that I was meant to play hockey and that was the main thing that I was focused on."[3] Bobby stood strong, stayed true, and set his own course.

Case Study: Sticking to Your Guns

"If you're passionate about something and stick with it, even if your friends aren't doing it, it'll pay off. It can be really rewarding to stick to your guns."
ELIZABETH GILLIES, actress

ONE OF THE most exceptional hockey players I have had the good fortune to work with stood out because he stuck to his

FINDING OUR OWN TRUE NORTH IS ESSENTIAL FOR ACCURATE NAVIGATION IN A WAY THAT'S RIGHT FOR US.

guns. Philadelphia Flyers director of hockey operations Chris Pryor said about player Brendan Ranford: "He's a smaller guy, those guys get underestimated. You look around the league and there're a lot of small guys playing and sometimes that happens."[4]

Consistently, Brendan has stuck to his guns in the face of other people's opinions, and consistently, he has worked on his game, his skating, his acceleration, his top-end speed, his mental performance—all the things that he knew would make him a better, more powerful hockey player. The key to Brendan's success is his determination to trust his gut, learn from others, and create a play that's all his own. "I don't really try and play like anyone, I try to play like myself, I try to take little things from different players who I watch, but everyone has their own style that they play," Brendan says.

He has amassed a wealth of powerful hockey achievements, including leading goal scorer and helping his team win the Calder Cup, all by sticking to his guns. Brendan has now been called up to the Dallas Stars. We can learn from his determination and focus, and accelerate our results by staying true to ourselves and our dreams.

As Henry David Thoreau said, "If one advances confidently in the direction of his dreams, and endeavors to live the life, which he has imagined, he will meet with a success unexpected." Our daydreams are powerful influencers that affect our results. Herb Brooks, who coached Team USA to Olympic gold in 1980, knew the importance of our dreams to achieving a successful life. He said, "We should be dreaming. We grew up as kids having dreams, but now we're too sophisticated as adults, as a nation. We stopped dreaming. We should always have dreams."[5] The more you focus on your dreams and feel how magnificent it would be to achieve them, the more power you have to manifest them in your own reality.

Using Your Intuition

"Your inner voice, your instinct, knows everything. If you listen to what you know instinctively, it will always lead you down the right path."

HENRY WINKLER, actor

OUR INTERNAL GUIDANCE system—our intuition—and our feelings are the most reliable measures of how true to ourselves we are living our lives. Our internal guidance system provides us with a sense of direction. Our dreams, our goals, and our desires are powerful. Being able to tune in to our intuition multiplies this power and helps us become mentally strong and focused. Our intuition is also known as our inner wisdom. We connect to our inner wisdom, our intuition, by paying close attention to how we feel. Every time we feel at ease and calm, we are receiving—without exception—communication from our intuition, letting us know we are on the right path. When we make a choice that we feel quietly, truly content, comfortable, and confident about, we are connecting to our intuition. If we feel at ease with our decision, then it is the right one for us at that time. We are following our own true north. The rule that I live by is: If making a choice makes me feel uneasy, then I need more information before I find that place of ease that tells me that I'm making the right choice.

When he was asked about his plans nearing the end of his career, superstar forward Jaromir Jagr said, "I play hockey because it makes me very happy. People retire and it's great and then five months later they don't know what to do. What are the chances I will find something else that will make me that happy?" [6] Now with his eighth NHL team, he has made the choice to keep playing. As author and actress Amber Riley says, "As long as you are being true to yourself, you will always find happiness." [7] Tuning in to your intuition makes you self-aware so that you can increase your personal power.

Your Personal Power

"At the center of your being you have the answer;
you know who you are and you know what you want."
LAO TZU, ancient Chinese philosopher

AS YOU HAVE been working through this book day by day, you will have experienced shifts in your self-awareness. Just the slightest opening of awareness can cause a shift in how you experience the world. As you become more aware of the impact of your thoughts on your life, your perception of reality has already shifted and your ability to strengthen your personal power has increased. Psychologist Daniel Goleman says, "If your emotional abilities aren't in hand, if you don't have self-awareness, if you are not able to manage your distressing emotions, if you can't have empathy and have effective relationships, then no matter how smart you are, you are not going to get very far."[8]

Being self-aware is the key to developing your mental strength, and it's the key to developing your hockey confidence. When you understand yourself better, you become aware of your strengths and of how to improve areas that you are not yet strong in. This means that you get to be in charge of your self-development, your self-empowerment. You will attract new opportunities so that you begin to become happier and more hockey confident.

Our daydreams are powerful influencers that affect our results.

When he was asked about the players he admires, Wayne Gretzky talked about the importance of self-awareness in hockey. He said, "The guy that I'm a little biased about, but the guy I think has hockey sense to only Crosby and [Brad]

Richards in New York is Kyle Turris. His hockey awareness and hockey sense is close to those two guys, and I consider them to have the best hockey sense in the game today. He's going to fit into that category soon."[9] Self-awareness is the key to the development of personal power and the key to the results of champions worldwide. And champions know how to ask for help when they need it, seeking out good role models and mentors for guidance and support.

Asking for Help

"What you want in a mentor is someone who truly cares for you and who will look after your interests and not just their own. When you do come across the right person to mentor you, start by showing them that the time they spend with you is worthwhile."

VIVEK WADHWA, entrepreneur

THE MOST SUCCESSFUL people know when they need help, and they ask for it. Mentors, teachers, and guides can help us save time and energy becoming the best person and the best player we know we can be.

As a hockey player, you have the ability to be always learning and growing. After taking on a bigger role with the Philadelphia Flyers than he had with his old team, the Toronto Maple Leafs, defenseman Luke Schenn welcomed all-star Chris Pronger's mentorship. "He's been helping me out since

Givers gain, and that gain shows up in mental strength and good results.

the start of training camp," Schenn acknowledged, adding, "I've still got a ton to learn."[10]

The key is to look for those who have dedicated themselves to their hockey; learn what you can from them by reading about them, watching them, or talking to them; and follow their good example to jumpstart your own journey. This will enhance your ability to maintain composure and stick to what is truly best for you—following your own true north. Then you, too, can boost your mental strength, confidence, and personal power by helping others in turn.

Givers Gain

"Simple acts of kindness, such as giving to charity or expressing gratitude, have a positive effect on our long-term moods. The key to the happy life, it seems, is the good life, a life with sustained relationships, challenging work, and connections to community.

PAUL BLOOM, professor of psychology and cognitive science

WHEN WE TAKE the time to look after our own well-being, develop a strong sense of self, and follow our own path, we have more energy and we find that it's easier to help others. When we help others, we develop powerful and rewarding relationships. Building those relationships is key to developing ourselves, our mental energy, our hockey ability, our confidence, and our personal power.

When Pittsburgh Penguins star Chris Kunitz was asked about the chemistry he has with his linemates Sidney Crosby and Pascal Dupuis, he said, "I think we all enjoy each other's company and humor. We can rib each other about certain things and that just picks us up. That's a hockey-player thing. It doesn't matter if you haven't seen guys in a while, we have that bond."[11] Being in sync with a superstar like Crosby has paid huge dividends to Kunitz, including two Olympic gold medals.

If you want good friends, you have to be a good friend. If you want to have great support to develop your hockey game, provide support to others—it pays off. Givers gain, and that gain shows up in mental strength and good results. "It doesn't matter if you're the smartest person in the room: If you're not someone who people want to be around, you won't get far," says screenwriter Melissa Rosenberg.[12]

Each of us has the power to influence another person and encourage them to be a better, more confident version of themselves. That goodwill reflects well on us and helps us develop a place of mental strength and happiness from which our best play can come. As it says in *Aesop's Fables*, "No act of kindness, no matter how small, is ever wasted."

Up-and-coming Colorado Avalanche star Matt Duchene showed that an act of kindness can profoundly affect another person. He helped a father win an autographed jersey at a charity auction for his bullied little girl. When the bidding went above the dollar amount the dad had scraped together, Matt told him, "Get it for her... I've got you covered,"[13] taking care of the cost of the cherished sweater himself.

Do you think that little girl will ever forget what Duchene's random act of kindness felt like? Do you think that Duchene felt good because he was able to help with a generous gift? It's a win-win. Helping someone else powers up both participants mentally and feels good all round.

Be Infectious!

"Belief in oneself is incredibly infectious. It generates momentum, the collective force of which far outweighs any kernel of self-doubt that may creep in."

AIMEE MULLINS, athlete, actor, and double amputee

A SMILE, LIKE a yawn, is infectious! A good mood, a positive outlook, is infectious. A desire to develop our mental strength, our desire to develop a stronger team, that's infectious. The right vibe, a good energy, a determination to grow and help others—these are key qualities of some of the greatest NHL players.

This is why some players are picked to play for the team and some are passed over. Garnet "Ace" Bailey played 568 solid games in the NHL before being killed in one of the planes from the September 11 attacks. One of the reasons he's so missed is his infectious personality. Sportscaster Mike Milbury, who played for the Boston Bruins like Ace Bailey, says, "If Ace were a wine he'd be champagne—bubbly. He was completely effervescent all the time, he always had a smile, always wanted to have fun, completely full of life."[14]

A positive personality can make or break a team. Those upbeat hard workers are often sources of inspiration, too, and that's powerful.

Be Inspiring!

"Hockey is a unique sport in the sense that you need each and every guy helping each other and pulling in the same direction to be successful."
WAYNE GRETZKY, hockey legend

IN CHAPTER 6, you learned about the importance of inspiring yourself to do your best and of being inspired by others to be greater.

It's just as crucial to be a source of inspiration for others. For every person you admire in hockey, you can be sure that there will be others who look at you in a similar way. Think of players who are younger than you, less experienced, less skilled. All of these players are looking to develop the same skills that you have. They watch you, they learn from you, they want to do what you do, and you can be the person to inspire them to do better. It benefits both of you.

Although Jim Kyte is legally deaf, he made himself a student of the game and played 598 NHL games as a tough, able defenseman. Kyte has been active in charities related to hearing impairments, including a summer hockey camp for hearing-impaired children. "Sport is a great vehicle for building confidence, particularly in children," he says.[15] Kyte used his experience with personal challenges to become his best self and inspire and work with others.

Being your best self serves as an example to others, inspires them, and encourages them to shine and then do the same for others. It's not only younger people you can inspire, it's also people on your team—and it will benefit you in return. In the words of actress Amy Poehler: "Find a group of people who challenge and inspire you, spend a lot of time with them, and it will change your life."[16]

A positive personality can make or break a team.

The greatest hockey teams thrive from the collective support of the players, the coaches, the whole organization, including the office staff, the fans, the sponsors, the media supporters, and of course, the families of the players. When the team works together, the results can be exceptional. Developing and nurturing deep relationships with linemates on the ice is worth the investment of time it takes. Toronto Maple Leafs players Lanny McDonald and Darryl Sittler developed a special chemistry, and "that friendship just blossomed into something that has lasted a lifetime," says McDonald.[17]

Who will you invest time and energy in today to develop an easy friendship and superb on-ice connection with? We can choose wisely and reap the rewards of building a legacy of friendship. In the words of the sixth president of the United States, John Quincy Adams: "If your actions inspire others to dream more, learn more, do more and become more, you are a leader."[18]

Your Legacy

"It is up to us to live up to the legacy that was left for us, and to leave a legacy that is worthy of our children and of future generations."
CHRISTINE GREGOIRE, American politician

IT'S IMPOSSIBLE TO walk along a beach without leaving footprints in the sand. In life, in hockey, too, it's impossible for us to take steps day by day without affecting others. The greatest players in the NHL are aware that each day their thoughts and actions can positively influence another person and leave a legacy of goodwill and inspiration. Each time we help another person, each time we share our learning, we leave a legacy that we can be proud of.

Pittsburgh Penguins number one draft pick Mario Lemieux played his way into the Hall of Fame and has dealt with cancer and an irregular heartbeat, but he has built his life into an impressive legacy every step of the way. He has no intention

of slowing down, stating, "I'm always going to be a Penguin...
I'd love to be involved in the franchise,"[19] in reference to his
desire to help the organization grow and to leave a legacy.

What is the legacy you want to be remembered for? Each
day, with every step we take, we have the opportunity to inspire
someone else, show kindnesses, and help
them develop their play. Both can benefit,
and both can leave a legacy of goodwill and
support as both take a step forward to reach
their goals.

Choose wisely and reap the rewards of building a legacy of friendship.

The only person who ultimately knows
what's best for you is you. The only person who
can fully understand what it feels like to be
you is you. By being true to you—your needs,
your dreams, and your goals—you build the
energy and the desire to help others achieve their dreams.
Three-time Stanley Cup champion Mark Recchi and many others took the time to encourage me to write this book to help
you follow your true north. That's my legacy for you, here in
this book.

It is with a strong mind and happy heart that I have shared
the tools, tips, stories, and words of inspiration that will help
you develop your mental performance, your skill, and your
love of hockey. Over the course of this book, you have been
able to build your self-awareness, your self-empowerment,
and your mental strength. You have been able to develop ways
of understanding and helping others, and you have traveled
from a place of needing inspiration to a place where you are

an inspiration. Your legacy is to take the learning from this book and use it, share it, look for ways to develop your mental performance each and every day, and pass on the good energy, the many ways that will help you develop your hockey game, and most of all, your hockey confidence.

Tips

1. Find your own true north to navigate life in a way that's right for you.

2. Be true to yourself and your dreams.

3. Develop your intuition by paying attention to how you feel.

4. Self-awareness is the key to the development of personal power.

5. Ask for help and choose your mentors wisely.

6. Power up yourself by helping others.

7. Be infectious—a positive personality can make or break a team.

8. Be a source of inspiration for others.

9. Leave a legacy that you are proud of.

AFTERWORD

HOCKEY: YOUR CONFIDENCE, YOUR DREAMS, YOUR RESULTS

Playing the Game of Your Life

PICTURE THIS...

Your heart is pounding.

The crowd is exploding, screaming your name. You are playing the game of your life.

Again and again, you hear your name—it becomes an anthem.

The anthem gets louder. The sound vibrates through your chest. It becomes a war cry.

The clock is running down. The team is watching you, trusting your every move.

You are in complete control. This is *your* time. The opposition is nothing more than a mere distraction. You know that you have the resources to deal with whatever twists of fate the gods throw at you tonight.

You feel your heart banging against your rib cage. You are sucking in air. You are smiling. You have learned from the best. You know how they faced their challenges. You are ready to stand on the shoulders of giants and take action.

You smell the sweat that's built up over the years seeping out of your hockey gear, its presence somehow reassuring.

You. Are. Beyond. Confident.

You are taking full responsibility for your personal success.

You inhale the frozen air coming off the ice. It reminds you of all the years you've spent flying from one end of the rink to the other. This is *your* ice.

You are solid, stable, balanced. Ready to set yourself on fire and take off.

You see the image of a cheetah in your mind's eye—dangerous, fully focused, and ready to explode at any second with controlled aggression. You know that you, and you alone, are responsible for your mood and you feel good.

You are ready to stand on the shoulders of giants and take action.

This is your time. You are truly confident.

This is your game. You are your own head coach. You speak well to yourself and you watch for the opportunities that you know are there.

You are playing the game of your life!

Then, in the time it takes to power a puck from one end of the ice to the other, you hear, "What the hell did you do that for?! You are an *idiot*!"

Within seconds, that hockey dream is now your worst nightmare.

The puck turns over. The other team is running away with your vision, your mission, and your future. Anxiety rears its ugly head. You snap right back down to earth—*bang*!

You immediately refocus your mental energy on your ABIL-ITY to skate like the wind and easily you reclaim your prize. You have your recovery strategies ready.

Your mind is strong. You know how powerful you are. You love to show your strength, your fast feet, your quick hands, your tenacity, and your skill.

You are the hunter. The other team is your prey.

You hear one of them chirp at you. You know how rattled the other team is that you are playing the game of your life. You sense that the way that player is talking to you is the way that he talks to himself. His mental nutrition leaves him hungry for moral support. You recognize his internal weakness and use it to your advantage.

The hand that gripped the hockey stick way too tight when you heard him chirp relaxes now, and you sense he's floundering inside.

The active relaxation technique gets you back into the flow, and you feel your self-esteem deepen as you ride the emotional wave of the game like a champion surfer.

Face-off. Two players. Same situation. Different results. The puck bounces unexpectedly. You were already waiting for the opportunity, the curve ball, to show up. You are there even before the other player realizes the puck has shot straight past him.

The pressure is on. You feel your lungs tighten. You take a second between shifts on the ice to check your breath health. You exhale, and you smile. You know that luck is yours for the taking.

All around you your team, your fans are looking up to you, complimenting you on your strength and focus. You expect to find ways to supercharge your results. You lift your game. You inspire your teammates. You soar high and land solid. Your coach is smiling. He knows you've got this.

Suddenly you realize how much your linemates are connecting with you. Your attitude to the game gives them the feeling of confidence.

You judge the game well. You are calm and alert, strong and focused, and you smile to yourself knowing how much more you have to give.

The result changes. Your team is now fully back in control. This is *our* ice. This is our game. This is our time!

You are standing strong, setting your course, and sticking to your guns. You are leading the team to trust themselves and their split-second decisions. Your strong mind is powering up the play of the whole team. You know that your self-discipline is causing the other team to make mistakes. You are truly and deeply confident in your own ability.

All too quickly, the game is over.

Your opponent's dreams lie smashed on the ice. Their hearts are aching, their heads pounding.

You hear the crowd ... cheering!

Your eyes glaze over and you can't even see your own stick clearly.

FACE-OFF.
TWO PLAYERS.
SAME SITUATION.
DIFFERENT RESULTS.

You are so proud of leading your team to this!

When you felt you were finally getting to the stage where you could be confident, trust your own instincts, and feel trusted, you stepped up and showed your true colors. Where once there was a fleeting feeling of confidence, there is now a steely strength that puts the feeling of fear into the other team.

You are living proof that when you take action, the right action, when you take one step a day in the right direction toward becoming stronger, fitter, faster, more accurate, and more confident, you get results.

This is your time, this is your game, and this is your life.

Those results may have happened slowly at first, just as when you first stepped out onto the ice all those years ago. But you quickly built momentum—first one foot, then the other; one thought, then another—and quickly you saw yourself making the shifts and changes you needed to become a better person, a better player.

A winner.

This is your time, this is your game, and this is your life. You have stood on the shoulders of the hockey giants, and you have learned from the best.

You have reached higher, skated faster, developed your focus and accuracy, got consistently confident, and become the champion you were meant to be.

You have left a legacy that every player dreams of. You have inspired others. You have powered up your performance by powering up your mind. You have trained your brain as much as you have trained your muscles, and the hard work has paid off.

You are now hockey confident.

NOTES

Introduction

1. Mike Johnston and Ryan Walter, *Simply the Best: Players on Performance* (Victoria, B.C.: Heritage House Publishing, 2007), 16.

One

1. "Mooseheads Beat Winterhawks 7–4 Saturday at MasterCard Memorial Cup," official site of the Ontario Hockey League, May 18, 2013, www.ontariohockeyleague.com/article/ mackinnon-leads-halifax-past-portland.
2. "DiabetesCare.net Interview: T1 Diabetes Never Stopped NHL Legend Bobby Clarke," DiabetesCare.net, October 8, 2010, www.diabetescare.net/article/title/diabetescarenet-interview-t1- diabetes-never-stopped-nhl-legend-bobby-clarke.
3. David Young, *Breakthrough Power for Athletes: A Daily Guide to an Extraordinary Life* (Wind Rock, TX: Wind Runner Press, 2011), 336.
4. Arnold H. Glasow, *Glasow's Gloombusters* (Freeport, IL: Gloombuster, 1995).
5. Joseph J.R. Mattera, *Think For Your Self: With Inspirational Words* (Bloomington, IN: AuthorHouse, 2015), 48.
6. Jean Ator, "What's It Like to Go to the Olympics with Your Twin?" *Women's Health*, February 19, 2014, www.womenshealthmag.com/life/ monique-lamoureux-and-jocelyne-lamoureux.

7. Chris Adalikwu, *How to Build Self Confidence, Happiness and Health* (Bloomington, IN: AuthorHouse, 2012), 108.

8. Ted Lindsay interview, Caregiver Solutions, accessed February 2014, www.caregiversolutions.ca.

9. Dan Goldstein, "The Battle between Your Present and Future Self," Ted Talk, November 2011, www.ted.com/talks/daniel_goldstein_the_battle_between_your_present_and_future_self/transcript?language=en.

Two

1. Thor Josefson, "Hockey Train's Top 10: Hockey Quotes of All Time," Hockey Train, February 16, 2012, accessed May 12, 2016, site. hockeytrain.com/blog/hockeytrains-top-10-hockey-quotes-of-all-time.

2. Mike Zeisberger, "Swedish Goaltender Henrik Lundqvist Says It's 'Stupid' to Focus on Anything Negative," *Toronto Sun*, February 21, 2014, www.torontosun.com/2014/02/21/swedish-goaltender-henrik-lundqvist-says-its-stupid-to-focus-on-anything-negative.

3. Rob Longley, "Longley on Team Canada: 'Where Is the Progress?'" *Toronto Sun*, February 16, 2014, www.torontosun.com/2014/02/16/longley-on-team-canada-where-is-the-progress.

4. Kara Leverte Farley and Sheila M. Curry, *Get Motivated! Daily Psych-Ups* (New York: Fireside, 1994), 10.

5. Christopher Ralph, "Wayne Gretzky and His Ridiculous Stats & Records Remain Timeless & Untouchable Even as 99 Turns 50," Hockey Writers, January 26, 2011, thehockeywriters.com/wayne-gretzky-and-his-ridiculous-stats-records-remain-timeless-untouchable-even-as-99-turns-50.

6. John O'Leary, "How Heroes Speak," John O'Leary Inspires, April 11, 2013, johnolearyinspires.com/2013/04/how-heroes-speak.

7. Joan Chittister, *Scarred by Struggle, Transformed by Hope* (Grand Rapids, MI: Eerdmans, 2003), 77.

Three

1. Don Miguel Ruiz, *The Four Agreements: A Practical Guide to Personal Freedom* (San Rafael, CA: Amber-Allen Publishing, 1997), 85.

2. Pierre LeBrun, "It's More than Luck for Niedermayer," ESPN, November 10, 2013, espn.go.com/nhl/story/_/id/9923904/2013-hockey-hall-fame-winning-followed-scott-niedermayer.

3. "Brandon Reid, Today's Notable Young Professional," Notable.ca, December 12, 2013, accessed February 2014, notable.ca/brandon-reid-todays-notable-young-professional.

4. David Feschuk, "Goal-Scoring Remains Leafs' 'Impossible' Dream: Feschuk," *Toronto Star*, November 6, 2015, accessed May 12, 2016, www.thestar.com/sports/leafs/2015/11/06/goal-scoring-remains-leafs-impossible-dream-feschuk.html.

5. "Steve Yzerman, St-Louis, Drake named to Order of Hockey in Canada," Canadian Press, CBC Sports, January 29, 2014, www.cbc.ca/sports/hockey/nhl/steve-yzerman-st-louis-drake-named-to-order-of-hockey-in-canada-1.2515911.

6. Don Miguel Ruiz, *The Four Agreements: A Practical Guide to Personal Freedom* (San Rafael, CA: Amber-Allen Publishing, 1997), 27.

7. Mark Newman, "Cory Emmerton Is Determined to Take His Career Day-by-Day and Continue to Prove That He Can Be a Valuable Two-Way Player at the NHL Level," Grand Rapids Griffins, January 30, 2014, accessed February 2014, griffinshockey.com/news/griffiti/?article_id=2719&content_type=printable&plugin_id=news.front.system&block_id=5005.

8. Napoleon Hill, *Think and Grow Rich* (La Vergne, TN: Lightning Source, 2009).

9. Mark Fischel, "Hockey's Future Interview with Jay Bouwmeester," Hockey's Future, April 4, 2002, www.hockeysfuture.com/articles/2777/hockeys_future_interview_with_jay_bouwmeester.

10. *Uncle John's Bathroom Reader: Shoots and Scores* (Vancouver: Raincoast Books, 2005), 66.

Four

1. Allen Mclaughlin, *The Tiger Woods Handbook: Everything You Need to Know about Tiger Woods* (Emereo Publishing, 2016).

2. Shawna Richer, *The Kid: A Season with Sidney Crosby and the New NHL* (Toronto: McClelland & Stewart, 2007), 28.

3. "Wayne Gretzky Biography," Biography.com, accessed May 10, 2016, http://www.biography.com/people/wayne-gretzky-9320468.

4. *Uncle John's Bathroom Reader: Shoots and Scores* (Vancouver: Raincoast Books, 2005), 98.

5. Rosanna Greenstreet, "Diddy: The Q&A," *Guardian*, June 21, 2008, accessed May 12, 2016, www.theguardian.com/music/2008/jun/21/urban.

6. "Famous Quotes," Texas Aces, accessed Feb 2014, texasaceshockey.com/Page.asp?n=2923.

7. Michelle Crechiolo, "Sutter Looking Forward to Playing Wing," NHL, January 15, 2014, penguins.nhl.com/club/news.htm?id=700834.

Five

1. Bill Potrecz, "Ellis a Study in Determination," *St. Catharine's Standard*, February 27, 2014, www.stcatharinesstandard.ca/2014/02/27/ellis-a-study-in-determination.

2. Ryan Walter, accessed February 2014, ryanwalter.com.

3. Bernie Parent, "Make Your New Year Resolution," Philly, accessed February 2014, www.philly.com.

4. Chris Lund, "Coach MacLean Post-Game," January 2, 2014, NHL, senators.nhl.com/club/blogpost.htm?id=24642.

5. Fluto Shinzawa, "Milan Lucic Led Way for Bruins in Playoffs," *Boston Globe*, June 27, 2013, www.bostonglobe.com/sports/2013/06/26/milan-lucic-led-way-for-bruins-playoffs/QuqQESYOJDerLJLSbROUFN/story.html.

6. Joseph A. Primm, *Live the Journey* (Searcy, AZ: Resource Publications, 2010), 184.

7. Henrik Edberg, "Wayne Gretzky's Top 3 Tips for Becoming the Best You Can Be," Positivity Blog, accessed February 2014, www.positivityblog.com/index.php/2009/06/12/wayne-gretskys-top-3-tips-for-becoming-the-best-you-can-be.

Six

1. Bob Foltman, "Evanston Native Gerald Coleman Bounced from Sport to Sport before Falling for Hockey, and the NHL's Diversity Program Has Helped Him," *Chicago Tribune*, June 26, 2003, articles.chicagotribune.com/2003-06-26sports/0306260353_1_ontario-hockey-league-nhl-diversity-playing.

2. Arash Markazi, "They Were Kings," ESPN, June 4, 2012, espn.go.com/los-angeles/nhl/story/_/id/7998050/in-1993-were-kings-los-angeles.

3. Sidney Crosby, Athletes, NBC Olympics, accessed February 2014, i.nbcolympics.com/athletes/athlete=2383/qa/index.html.

4. Rachel Corrie, *Let Me Stand Alone: The Journals of Rachel Corrie* (New York: W.W. Norton, 2009).

5. James Mirtle, "Nazem Kadri and Dallas Eakins Square off in Edmonton," *Globe and Mail*, October 29, 2013, www.theglobeandmail.com/sports/hockey/leafs-beat/nazem-kadri-and-dallas-eakins-square-off-in-edmonton/article15138694.

6. "Transcript: Michelle Obama's Convention Speech," NPR, September 4, 2012, www.npr.org/2012/09/04/160578836/transcript-michelle-obamas-convention-speech.

7. Robert Tychowski, "New Edmonton Oilers Defenceman Andrew Ference Says Team Can Only Succeed if Everyone's Pulling in the Same Direction," *Edmonton Sun*, July 16, 2013, www.edmontonsun.com/2013/07/16/new-edmonton-oilers-defenceman-andrew-ference-says-team-can-only-succeed-if-everyones-pulling-in-the-same-direction.

8. Dejan Kovacevic, "Penguins? James Neal Visualizes, Realizes Goals," Trib Live, December 25, 2011, triblive.com/x/pittsburghtrib/sports/penguins/s_773691.html#axzz2shipfmdf.

Seven

1. Lesley Sheppard, "Quotes from Theoren Fleury's Interview with the *Times-Herald*," *Moose Jaw Times-Herald*, October 20, 2009, www.mjtimes.sk.ca/News/2009-10-20/article-135577/ Quotes-from-Theoren-Fleurys-interview-with-the-Times-Herald/1.

2. Jack Canfield, "Two Secrets to a Better You," Huff Post Health Living, November 17, 2011, accessed May 12, 2016, www.huffingtonpost.com/ jack-canfield/two-secrets-to-a-better-y_b_268590.html.

3. "Jaromir Jagr Quote," accessed February 2014, Yahoo! Sports, ca.sports.yahoo.com.

4. Jonathan Willis, "Pat Quinn by Quotes," Oilers Nation, August 4, 2009, oilersnation.com/2009/8/4/pat-quinn-by-quotes.

5. Neha Gandhi, "Meet *90210*'s Tristan Wilds," *Seventeen*, October 26, 2011, accessed May 12, 2016, www.seventeen.com/celebrity/a16611/ tristan-wilds-interview.

6. Tim Wharnsby, "Hunters Jousted to Create Knights," *Globe and Mail*, December 13, 2004, www.theglobeandmail.com/sports/ hunters-jousted-to-create-knights/article18279327.

7. Bill Roose, "Babcock Says Players Must Relax," NHL, November 20, 2013, redwings.nhl.com/club/news.htm?id=692475&cmpid= rssroose&utm_source=dlvr.it&utm_medium=twitter.

8. Mike G. Morreale, "Nichushkin Tops List of Russian Stars in Traverse City," NHL, September 9, 2013, www.nhl.com/ice/ m_news.htm?id=681835.

9. Eric Duhatschek, "Canada Faces U.S. in Battle for Women's Hockey Olympic Gold" *Globe and Mail*, February 19, 2014, www.theglobeandmail.com/sports/olympics/new-role-for-wickenheiser-at-her-last-games/article16984589.

10. David Trifunov, "Boston Bruins, Buffalo Sabres Salute Hurting City after Marathon Bombings," Global Post, April 18, 2013, www.globalpost.com/dispatches/globalpost-blogs/world-at-play/ boston-bruins-buffalo-sabres-salute-hurting-city-after-mar.

Eight

1. Mike Davies, "Smith Destined to Play Hockey," *Peterborough Examiner*, November 19, 2008, www.trentonian.ca/2008/11/18/ smith-destined-to-play-hockey.

2. John Wooden and Steve Jamison, *Wooden: A Lifetime of Observations and Reflections On and Off the Court* (New York: McGraw-Hill Education, 1997).

3. Jack Batten, *The Leafs in Autumn* (Toronto: MacMillan, 1975), 18.

4. Larry Lage, "US Hopes Maturing Kane Can Help Win Gold in Sochi," AP, January 24, 2014, wintergames.ap.org/article/us-hopes-maturing-kane-can-help-win-gold-sochi.

5. Casey Lewis, "Lea Michele on Sororities, Self-Care, and Her On-Set BFF Emma Roberts," *Teen Vogue*, September 21, 2015, accessed May 12, 2016, www.teenvogue.com/storylea-michele-journal-scream-queens-emma-roberts.

6. Mark Newman, "Pulling No Punches," November 25, 2008, Grand Rapids Griffins, accessed May 12, 2016, griffinshockey.com/news/griffiti/?article_id=112.

7. "Wayne Gretzky Quotes," Brainy Quote, accessed February 2014, www.brainyquote.com/quotes/authors/w/wayne_gretzky.html.

Nine

1. Tabatha Coffey, "I Am a Bitch!" Huff Post Queer Voices, January 9, 2012, www.huffingtonpost.com/tabatha-coffey/i-am-a-bitch _b_1194001.html.

2. Lance Secretan, *Inspire! What Great Leaders Do* (New York: Wiley, 2010), 45.

3. Spencer Friedman, Interview, Orr: My Story, accessed February 2014, bobbyorrenglish.weebly.com/interview.html.

4. Dustin Leed, "Meet Flyers Prospect Brendan Ranford," Hockey Guys, December 7, 2010, thehockeyguys.net/meet-flyers-prospect-brendan-ranford.

5. "Coach Known Best for 1980 Hockey Gold," Associated Press, ESPN, August 19, 2003, accessed February 2014, espn.go.com/classic/obit/s/2003/0811/1594173.html.

6. Will Pakuta, "Jaromir Jagr Lighting It Up for the Devils as His Colorful Hockey Journey Winds Down," *New York Daily News*, January 25, 2014, www.nydailynews.com/sports/hockey/jagr-lighting-colorful-hockey-journey-winds-article-1.1591342.

7. "Amber Riley Biography," IMDB, accessed May 12, 2016, www.imdb.com/name/nm3232025/bio.

8. Neal F. Chalofsky, *Handbook of Human Resource Development* (New York: Wiley, 2014), 627.

9. Dan Rosen, "Five Questions: Gretzky Believes Kings Can Repeat," January 29, 2013, NHL, www.nhl.com/ice/m_news.htm?id=653065.

10. James Mirtle, "Schenn Finds a Perfect Mentor in Chris Pronger," *Globe and Mail*, April 5, 2013, www.theglobeandmail.com/sports/hockey/globe-on-hockey/schenn-finds-a-perfect-mentor-in-chris-pronger/article10823941.

11. Dan Rosen, "Five Questions: Kunitz on Life as Crosby's Linemate," NHL, October 22, 2013, www.nhl.com/news/five-questions-kunitz-on-life-as-crosbys-linemate/c-687791.

12. Sharon Lechter, *Think and Grow Rich for Women: Using Your Power to Create Success and Significance* (New York: Penguin, 2014).

13. Wayde Greer, "Colorado Avalanche Centre Matt Duchene's Random Act of Kindness Gives Ontario Girl Big Boost," *Toronto Sun*, August 8, 2013, www.torontosun.com/2013/08/08/colorado-avalanche-centre-matt-duchenes-random-act-of-kindness-gives-ontario-girl-big-boost.

14. "Bruins Alumni Remember Jokester Ace Bailey," NESN, March 13, 2010, nesn.com/2010/03/bruins-alumni-remember-jokester-ace-bailey.

15. "The Jim Kyte Story!" Hockey Family Advisor, accessed February 2014, hockeyfamilyadvisor.com/the-jim-kyte-story.

16. "You Can't Do It Alone," *Harvard Magazine*, May 25, 2011, accessed May 12, 2016, harvardmagazine.com/2011/05/you-cant-do-it-alone.

17. "One on One with Lanny McDonald," official site of the Hockey Hall of Fame, April 4, 2003, www.hhof.com/htmlSpotlight/spot_oneononep199204.shtml.

18. Thomas J. Wurtz, *Corporate Common Sense: Revolutionary Business Lessons Inspired by Thomas Paine* (Bloomington, IN: AuthorHouse, 2009), 256.

19. Robert Dvorchak, "Lemieux Says He Would Like to Stay in Mix," *Pittsburgh Post-Gazette*, October 6, 2006, www.post-gazette.com/sports/penguins/2006/10/06Lemieux-says-he-would-like-to-stay-in-mix/stories/200610060119.

ACKNOWLEDGMENTS

WRITING IS A SOLITARY action, yet the act of writing is made more rewarding by the support, the help, the stories, the care, and the love of family, friends, colleagues, and many, many hockey players. This wealth of riches has such an impact that this book would not have been possible without the following people:

There have been key people whose acts of kindness have, like a rogue puck, offered me the moment of opportunity that comes when we work with focus and belief. RCMP officer George Buttuls; NHL and WHL coach Guy Charron and his lovely wife, Michele; executive director of the Kamloops Blazers Angie Mercuri; and Billet Mom of all Billet Moms Kerry Rubel have all found ways to help me take one step closer to achieving the dream of helping hockey players to develop their confidence. Each is well loved and valued. Thank you for the support, cheeky words, and hugs that fueled the emotional energy that sustained the writing process.

There were the kindhearted Kamloopsians who took the time to talk, talk, talk hockey and share with me their passion for the game: Heinz Elbeck, who counseled "pleasant persistence," AKA "be the squeaky wheel...!" in my quest for support for this book; Parker Bennett, who took time out of his busy day to prep me for meeting some of the hockey greats; Robyn and Shawn Haley, who taught me how to love hockey with a fierce pride for my team; and my lion heart, Kaz Farch, who took me to my first NHL game. Heinz and Kaz are no longer with us in person, so it is comforting to imagine both of them yelling at the big TV in the sky when their favorite teams, Vancouver and Calgary, are playing each other.

To my colleagues with kind hearts who read first drafts of the book, corrected my Welshisms, and took the time to ask their friends to support the book: Rob Nordin, Rob Shween, Tara Holmes, Stacey Gagnon. You make me smile, and you inspire me and many others in our local community. Thank you.

For the wordsmiths in the local media who saw the heart in this book and supported good intentions from a gal who was an unusual source of support for their beloved hockey team: Jon Keen, Rick "the Bear" Wile, Marty Hastings. Your passion for your team is conta-gious—Let's go, Blazers!

For the clients and parents of clients who became friends and stalwart supporters of my work and my writing: hockey players Cam Lanigan, Colin Smith, James Leonard, Brendan Ranford; Olympic skier Elli Terwiel; Aspen Open winner Emma Whitman; pro skier Brett Dawley; and golfer Ryan Weatherall. Thank you for sharing your stories, your time, and your trust.

True legends make their mark on and off the ice. Thank you to the NHL hockey legends whose encouragement and support made a powerful impact on this brain trainer: Doug Lidster, Corey Hirsch, Tom Renney, Mark Recchi, Darryl Sydor, Mark Kachowski, Riley Nash, and Jarome Iginla. I had to dig deep to find the confidence to reach out to each one of you. Thank goodness the confidence tools I needed to reach out to you were right in front of me! It's an honor to have received words of encouragement from the hockey greats. All of you, humble enough to help, talented enough to inspire. Thank you.

I have had the great fortune to have family members, my own and extended, who supported learning, love, and laughter. From my champion Jean-Pierre, to my stalwart nurturers Dom and Sue Szczepanski, to my quiet support Terry Smith, I say thank you for your kind words. They helped more than you may know.

For encouraging me to be happy in my nature, my rock stars Dr. Matt James, Dr. Patrick Scott, Aaron Le May, and the always elegant Cathy Ferguson; and my gentle and kind friends Sarah Thygesen, Karra Farch, Don Arney, and Victoria Rutherford.

For her kind words that I read every day that I'm in my office, my young cousin Sarah Szczepanski. For being my greatest brain trainer, and for showing me her kindness, determination, and how to become a stickler for getting great results, Beatrice Smith. Merci, Maman.

For their belief in the actualization of my dream to provide tools and techniques to build hockey confidence, my book agent Arnold Gosewich and publishing team at Greystone Books. A debt of gratitude to my exceptional editor, Shirarose Wilensky, who provided stalwart encouragement.

And finally, for the endless cups of tea it takes to write chapters for hours at a time, days at a time; for the cwtches that reignite the gentle energy inside at the end of a long, long day at the computer; and for understanding the power of solitude for a happy introvert... my seneschal William Dallimore. May we always follow our true north.

ABOUT THE AUTHOR

ISABELLE HAMPTONSTONE, MSc, is an Olympic and NHL confidence and performance expert and the creator of the Ultimate Confidence, Performance, and Inner Strength Technique™. She is the CEO of the award-winning Brain Train International, the Specialists in Confidence Inc., which helps professionals in business, elite sport, public service, and leadership positions increase performance with specific and measurable results. The company specializes in training brains to eliminate unhelpful thought patterns so they are more efficient and can optimize performance under pressure.

Isabelle lives in Sun Peaks, B.C. She was an air force cadet and a reservist officer in the British Army and became a glider pilot when she was 16 years old. Her ideal dinner party would include Jeremy Clarkson, Maharishi Mahesh Yogi, EDM's Steve Aoki, Taylor Swift, Queen Eleanor of Aquitaine, Joan of Arc, and Daniel Craig. Izzy dreams of driving a supercar in Germany's Nürburgring, just like the guys in Top Gear.

For more information on Isabelle's work or *Hockey Confidence,* visit www.braintrainconfidence.com.